The Women of

Smeltertown

SMELTERTOWN

THE KANSAS CITY CONSOLIDATED SMELTING AND REFINING COMPANY CAME TO EL PASO IN THE LATE 19TH CENTURY, CREATING A MINING AND SMELTING CENTER FOR THE SOUTHWEST. IN 1899, THE AMERICAN SMELTING AND REFINING COMPANY (ASARCO) BOUGHT THE OPERATION AND REFINED LEAD, COPPER AND OTHER ORES. THE NEED FOR A LARGE LABOR POOL BROUGHT IN THOUSANDS OF MEXICAN IMMIGRANTS; THESE WORKERS ESTABLISHED HOMES FOR THEIR FAMILIES ON COMPANY LAND AROUND THE SMELTER AND DEVELOPED A DYNAMIC COMMUNITY CALLED SMELTERTOWN, OR *LA ESMELDA*.

SMELTERTOWN GREW INTO A SMALL CITY WITHIN A CITY AND WAS HOME TO ASARCO BRICK AND CEMENT PLANTS, AND A LIMESTONE QUARRY. THE SETTLEMENT WAS DIVIDED INTO UPPER AND LOWER SMELTERTOWN, OR *EL ALTO* AND *EL BAJO*, AND WITHIN THESE AREAS WERE SMALLER BARRIOS. THE ONLY ONE REMAINING TODAY IS *LA CALAVERA*, OR SKULL CANYON, LAID OUT ALONG THE ROAD TO THE SMELTERTOWN CEMETERY. SMELTERTOWN WAS HOME TO ITS OWN Y.M.C.A. BRANCH AND SCHOOLS, MOST NOTABLY E.B. JONES SCHOOL. THROUGHOUT THE AREA, RESIDENTS ESTABLISHED ORGANIZATIONS, STORES, RESTAURANTS AND OTHER BUSINESSES, AND NAMED STREETS AFTER RESIDENTS WHO DIED IN MILITARY SERVICE DURING WORLD WAR II. THE SAN JOSÉ DEL RIO (SAN JOSÉ DE CRISTO REY CATHOLIC CHURCH) SERVED THE RESIDENTS AS A PLACE FOR WORSHIP AND SOCIAL AND COMMUNITY ACTIVITY. PARISHIONERS UNDERTOOK REGULAR PILGRIMAGES TO THE TOP OF *CERRO DE MULEROS*, NOW KNOWN AS MOUNT CRISTO REY, AND INITIATED CREATION OF THE CRISTO REY MONUMENT, ERECTED IN 1940.

IN THE EARLY 1970s, AFTER ENVIRONMENTAL OFFICIALS FOUND HIGH LEVELS OF LEAD CONTAMINATION IN THE SOIL, COMMUNITY BUILDINGS WERE RAZED AND FAMILIES WERE RELOCATED. TODAY, AN ANNUAL REUNION BRINGS FORMER RESIDENTS TOGETHER TO REMEMBER THE ONCE VIBRANT AND BUSTLING SMELTERTOWN.

(2006)

The Women of
Smeltertown

Marcia Hatfield Daudistel

Mimi R. Gladstein

Contemporary Photographs

by Carol Eastman

Foreword by Yolanda Chávez-Leyva

Afterword by Howard Campbell

Fort Worth, Texas

Library of Congress Cataloging-in-Publication Data

Names: Daudistel, Marcia Hatfield, author. | Gladstein, Mimi Reisel, author.
  | Eastman, Carol, photographer.
Title: The women of Smeltertown / Marcia Hatfield Daudistel, Mimi R.
  Gladstein ; contemporary photographs by Carol Eastman ; introduction by
  Yolanda Chavez-Leyva ; afterword by Howard Campbell.
Description: Fort Worth, Texas : TCU Press, [2018]
Identifiers: LCCN 2018023682 | ISBN 9780875657004 (alk. paper)
Subjects: LCSH: Mexican American women--Texas--Smeltertown--History. |
  Women--Texas--Smeltertown--History. | Community
  life--Texas--Smeltertown--History. | Collective
  memory--Texas--Smeltertown. | Smeltertown (Tex.)--Social conditions.
Classification: LCC F394.S64 D38 2018 | DDC 305.48/86872073076496--dc23
LC record available at https://urldefense.proofpoint.com/v2/url?u=https-3A__lccn.loc.
gov_2018023682&d=DwIFAg&c=7Q-FWLBTAxn3T_E3HWrzGYJrC4RvUoWDrz-
TlitGRH_A&r=O2eiy819IcwTGuw-vrBGiVdmhQxMh2yxeggw9qlTUDE&m=Kr7N-
Nd98fsNaJ6O-00iH088AorSIy5xRCzrEhjmDRuI&s=2Dnm3_Wyl3N7B9r9HcqV-
VWAsY70FthCVpa22UUhdvZM&e=

Benjamin Alire Sáenz's poem "The Blue I Loved" is from *Elegies in Blue:
Poems* (Cinco Puntos Press, 2002). Used by permission of the author.

Bryan Woolley's story "Rosa" is from *The Wonderful Room* (Wings Press,
2010). Reprinted by permission of the estate of Bryan Woolley.

Cover and text design by Elizabeth Cruce Alvarez, Southlake, Texas.

TCU Box 298300
Fort Worth, Texas 76129

www.prs.tcu.edu

To order books: 1.800.826.8911

*For the women and children of Smeltertown
who generously shared their family stories
and made this book possible.*

Contents

The Blue I Loved

Benjamin Alire Sáenz

Maria de Guadalupe Cenizeros, citizen of Smeltertown,
sings a lullaby explaining the color
of the headstone on her grave

I loved the August rains, I loved the calm October
days. I loved the sound of thunder as it echoed
in the nights; I loved the breeze that made my curtains
dance a waltz. I loved the water in the river,
chocolate as my skin.

I loved the smell of beans,
the smoothness of the masa in my hands. I loved
the stacks of fresh tamales on the stove, the
taste of yerba buena on my tongue. I loved
the rows of chile in the fields,

I loved the look on Mama's face
before she closed her eyes and never woke again.
I loved the worn wood rosary she left to me, her
only child to live past thirty years. I loved the
picture of her wedding day. I placed it next to mine.
I looked like her. That is what I loved: I had her
face, her eyes.

I loved the stove where I cooked meals
as simple as the wood I walked on with bare feet.
I loved those pisos made of wood, and loved the Little
Flower of Jesus. She made me hers. And just like me
she loved the smell of candles and copal. I loved
the afternoons we talked just she and I.

I loved to wake
the house each dawn. I loved my children's grumbling
as they rose to meet the sun. I loved their look
of hunger as they ate. I loved their loving me.
I loved their look of pain when I grew sick.
Their tears burned like the sun the day I died.
I loved my husband's eyes. Green
as apples growing on a branch. I loved his
hand upon my back. The roughness made me tremble.

Forty years that man could make me tremble.
He's buried next to me. In death I swear he snores.
We sleep the way we lived: in peace. And one
more thing I loved. I loved, I loved the color blue,
the color of the room where we made love and slept.
Where we made love and slept.
I loved the color blue.

From *Elegies in Blue: Poems*

Foreword

A hundred years ago, a thriving community grew around the American Smelting and Refining Company (ASARCO). The Rio Grande/Rio Bravo was broad and filled with water. The 1918 Land Reclamation Act that resulted in the construction of the Elephant Butte Dam had not yet diverted its water. The Smeltertown community claimed its own school, church, and cemetery. Almost two thousand people found their final resting place in the cemetery that served the community from 1882 to 1970. For more than a century, the two red and white towers marked the space. Today, Smeltertown no longer exists; the river is dry much of the year; and the towers have been demolished. Yet Smeltertown lives on in the memories of the people who lived there and in the stories passed on from generation to generation. It is not uncommon for people in El Paso to say, "My grandfather worked there" or "My mother was born there." The descendents of *los esmeltianos* (the residents of Smeltertown) may not know all the details of their families' histories, but they remember the connection. *The Women of Smeltertown* is a treasure trove of those stories told from the point of view of the women who made their lives there. Those whose family roots grew deep in Smeltertown soil, as well as those who want to better understand community-making, or borderlands and women's history, will welcome this book.

The contemporary US-Mexico borderline is more than 160 years old. The modern boundary line was shaped by a war between the United States and Mexico from 1846 to 1847 and the Gadsden Purchase in 1853. Even the once-powerful river helped configure the boundary as it shifted until it was finally stabilized through canalization in the 1960s. For much of its existence, the border has been the site of controversy and criticism as well as creativity and resilience. It is a place where national identity is questioned and reinforced. It is a place where cultures come together, sometimes in conflict, to create something new. It is a place where people, ideas, capital, and goods cross back and forth. Smeltertown is a result of this history. The stories in *The Women of Smeltertown* reveal this complex history in rich detail.

The economic expansion of the borderlands and the history of the two nations have been interwoven for two centuries. Beginning in the 1820s, US intervention in the Mexican north, both in Texas and New Mexico, transformed the region economically and demographically. The US-Mexico War of 1846 changed the history of both nations as Mexico lost half of its territory to the United States. By the 1880s, under the presidency of Porfirio Diaz in Mexico, and with the emergent economic development of the US Southwest, both sides of the border became increasingly tied together, bolstered by the movement of people south to north, and of capital north to south. Economic development came with the railroads and the emergence of commercial mining and agriculture. It was in this context that ASARCO and Smeltertown were born.

Early El Paso civic leaders touted El Paso as a perfect mining center. "Look out for big deals," declared the *El Paso Times* in 1900. They were right. The El Paso Smelter, founded 1889, joined with ASARCO in 1899. Over its history, ASARCO was associated with well-known financiers like the Rockefellers and the Guggenheims. Generations of Mexican Americans and Mexican immigrants worked at the smelter. By the early twentieth century, ASARCO represented the largest employer in the city, employing 1,500 men by 1903, according to *Desert Immigrants: The Mexicans of El Paso, 1880–1920.*

The men, however, were not alone. They brought their wives and families. Over the decades, the community grew, and even when people left, they remained tied to their smelter community. In 1970, the City of El Paso and the State of Texas filed a lawsuit against ASARCO, arguing that the company had violated the Texas Clean Air Act. Studies showed lead contamination in the soil and in the residents of Smeltertown, including seventy-two Smeltertown residents (approximately fifty percent of them children) who had lead poisoning. In 1975, Smeltertown was razed and the *esmeltianos* were forced to move. In 2013, the two towers were demolished.

For much of the twentieth century, El Paso served as the Ellis Island of the Southwest. As the major port of entry from Mexico into the United States, the city welcomed thousands of immigrants. They came seeking employment and better lives for their families. Early in the twentieth century, they came seeking refuge from the Mexican Revolution and its aftermath. El Paso was a railroad hub that connected the United States with Mexico, and its economic development revolved around mining, agriculture, and railroads. Low-paid ethnic Mexican laborers made the development possible.

As Mexican immigrants came to El Paso in the early twentieth century, often recruited by these industries, they developed communities that were stabilized by relationships between families, religious institutions and practices, and shared experiences. Women were at the heart of stabilizing communities. While women did work outside the home, often as laundresses and in garment factories, most ethnic Mexicans labored inside their homes. They worked as keepers and teachers of culture, nurturing their families both physically and emotionally. Women created homes out of sometimes crude structures, planting flowers to bring beauty to the landscape, saving to bring inside plumbing to their families, and putting down floors to cover the original dirt. The wives of ASARCO managers also helped create and maintain their own community, although separate from that of the ethnic Mexican community, hosting coffee klatches and carpooling their children to school.

The Women of Smeltertown is about community and it is about place. The two are intimately linked in the memories of the women in this book. The river, the desert, and the mountains define El Paso. So too, the contours of the land defined Smeltertown. *Esmeltianos* knew well the differences among Smelter Terrace, El Alto, La Calavera, and El Bajo. Smelter Terrace, with its elegant English-language name, was home to ASARCO's managers and their families. El Alto was high above El Bajo. La Calavera, named after Skull Canyon, and El Bajo were the locations of homes without indoor plumbing; even so, former residents remembered the beauty of the desert and their homes. As one resident, Ramiro Escandon, pointed out, "Mexican families care about their surroundings and their gardens." Dolores Romero remembered the beauty of the water going through the arroyo at La Calavera to the river. The love of place resonates throughout *The Women of Smeltertown*.

This book makes an important contribution to the literature on women and Mexican-American women in particular. Historians such as Vicki L. Ruiz have documented the lives of El Paso's women as they made their way in the United States. Describing the lives of Mexican women in the United States, Ruiz details their cultural, political, and economic contributions in the twentieth century. In an earlier historical monograph, *Desert Immigrants*, Mario T. Garcia depicts the lives of Mexican immigrants in the late nineteenth and early twentieth centuries, including the work of women inside and outside the home. In *Smeltertown: Making and Remembering a Southwest Border Community*, historian Monica Perales describes the ways in which gender shaped the experiences of Smeltertown's residents, *los esmeltianos*. Women directed *escuelas particulares*, small home-based schools where Mexican culture was taught and maintained. At the Smeltertown Vocational School, girls learned how to sew and how to dress. And young women rebelled against their more traditional parents as they adopted American culture.

The Women of Smeltertown builds on these studies and others. Its significance lies in the intimate histories told about building their community, from working in their kitchens to nurturing families and creating small food-centered businesses, to literally building the monument on Mount Cristo Rey by carrying rocks up the mountain in buckets. Based on oral histories, this book allows us to read the history of Smeltertown directly through the words of the women who lived there.

Oral history creates connections among people and across time. When oral history arrived on the academic scene in the1940s, critics said it was unreliable and that people's memories changed over time. While it is true that our memories can change as we grow older and the years pass, oral histories allow us to look at what is significant to people and the meaning they make from their experiences. Listening to, or in this case reading, the memories of individuals allows us to look intimately into their lives, but it also allows us to connect to them. The beauty and the struggles of day-to-day experiences jump off the pages of this book. One of the gifts of oral history is that it allows women to tell their stories on their own terms. As oral historians Sherna Berger Gluck and Daphne Patai have written in *Women's Words: The Feminist Practice of Oral History,* we must listen carefully to the women's stories. As they write, "We have to learn to listen in stereo, receiving both the dominant and muted channels clearly." The "muted channels" are revealed in the stories of women like Alicia Sarmiento Ramirez, who asked her husband to help her out around the home. Although initially angered by her request, she reported that later he became a good cook.

The photographs accompanying the chapters add visual depth to the oral histories. The combination of historic photographs with contemporary portraits by Carol Eastman brings life to the already poignant words of the interviewees. The photographs of young white children standing in front of a small lake or playing catch on a large manicured lawn provide us a powerful image of life in Smelter Terrace, while the image of a young Mexican American girl in her first communion dress gives texture to the stories of the Catholic church's influence on people's day-to-day lives. The land, too, is revealed in these photographs. Eastman's photograph of the ASARCO tower falling with Mount Cristo Rey in the background and the photo of the remaining white brick wall of San Jose Church show the changing landscape. The photograph of people gathering for a pilgrimage up Mount Cristo Rey equally reveals the enduring importance of memory. Finally, the portraits of the interviewees allow us to appreciate the passing of time and the emotions elicited by remembering.

As the authors Marcia Hatfield Daudistel and Mimi R. Gladstein write, "The spirit of the Smeltertown community is remarkable." That spirit is reflected in each page of the book through stories of hardship and good times. By focusing on the remembrances of Smeltertown's women, this book adds to the many layers of history and memory of a place that was once a significant symbol of the economic progress that played out in the lives of women, men, and children.

Yolanda Chávez-Leyva
The University of Texas at El Paso

Acknowledgments

The *Women of Smeltertown* was made possible through the support of people who believed in this project from the beginning. Foremost are the interviewees who welcomed us into their homes to share their memories, family stories, and photographs. They often led us to other women and families with stories to tell. They are named in the book.

We were honored to be included in the Zubia family tamalada. In the process of learning how to assemble dozens and dozens of tamales for the holidays, we were included in a traditional family event centered around the women of the family. It was a very special experience.

It became obvious early in the project that the stories we heard must be preserved. The women and their families lived in an environment that most of El Paso knew nothing about. During the decades they lived in Smeltertown and raised families, sweeping social change affected the traditional roles of women. They were frequently ahead of their time in their full-time employment outside the home and their strong emphasis on education for their children. A strong community of extended family and friends developed that was not the nuclear family portrayed in mainstream media.

Beto Lopez, Assistant Vice President of Institutional Advancement at The University of Texas at El Paso, whose father ran the Smeltertown YMCA, was an early and important source, introducing us at the annual Smeltertown Reunion and providing valuable contacts. Rosa Guerrero, an El Paso Folklorico icon, was also a valuable resource. Early in our research Holli Berry put us in touch with some out-of-town interviewees, including the women raised in Smelter Terrace, who had never told their stories before. Martha Lou Broaddus led us to several sources connected to the educational world.

Claudia Rivers, head of Special Collections at the University of Texas at El Paso Library, was invaluable in assisting Carol Eastman with photo research and providing permission for use of the historical photographs. Claudia's encyclopedic knowledge of El Paso history makes any research easier. Thanks also to Vianey Aldarete, our UTEP research assistant, for her invaluable help.

We also thank our friend Bobbi Gonzales, who provided expert transcription of the interviews. Dan Williams, Melinda Esco, and Kathy Walton of TCU Press continue to make the transformation from manuscript to book an enjoyable one. They are a pleasure to work with from submission to final project.

Marcia Hatfield Daudistel
Mimi R. Gladstein

Smelter towers falling, 2013. *Photo by Carol Eastman.*

Introduction

In the early morning of April 1, 2013, all of El Paso waited in anticipation. Traffic on I-10 was stopped going both east and west. Citizens congregated in the most advantageous viewing sites on the mesas and hills near the towers of ASARCO. After months of conflict and heated argument over whether or not the stacks should be preserved, those in favor were unable to raise the money to maintain them, so the 612-foot stack and the 828-foot stack, once the tallest in the world, were demolished in ten seconds. Even the *Wall Street Journal* reported on this momentous occasion. A collective cheer went up from the crowd and from those watching the demolition at home on television.

To many, those mammoth smokestacks were the last reminder of the clouds of emissions that came from the smelter. Former students at Texas Western College, now the University of Texas at El Paso, remembered the clouds of pollution the wind frequently failed to dissipate permeating the campus in the 1950s. As late as the 1980s, even at night, the dark orange smoke was visible along the interstate. Drivers and passengers could taste copper in their mouths.

Smeltertown was an insular community that even native and long-time El Paso residents were rarely familiar with. The negative impact of the demolition on the former residents was not felt by the many who had only driven by ASARCO.

Not everyone celebrated the toppling of the mammoth smoke-stacks. There were generations of families who lived in their shadow. Great-grandparents fleeing the Mexican Revolution, those looking for a chance at a better life, and those born in the houses surrounding ASARCO were part of the history of a community. For the now-adult children who lived in those houses with their grandmothers, mothers, and aunts—women who created strong families and a vibrant community—memories of life there are happy ones. Although the homes were torn down in 1972, the towers were the last visible symbol of the lives they lived in Smeltertown.

Once there was a place called Smeltertown, and it was known as the largest industrial city on the banks of the Rio Grande. The distinctive red-and-white-striped smokestacks grew so tall over the decades that they became landmarks just inside the US side of the border. A community of small adobe houses on unpaved dirt roads, named only by a letter of the alphabet, developed across the road from the smelter, occupied mainly by the workers employed by the American Smelting and Refining Company (ASARCO) and their extended families. The smelter did not own the homes; they were owned by individual landlords, so employment at ASARCO was not a requirement. Lacking indoor plumbing, many with dirt floors, these homes were located in the area called El Bajo, the low. More immediate to the smelter was an area owned by the company called El Alto, the high, reflecting its geographic location. The larger modern homes for the management and their families, in that same area but separated from El Alto, were called Smelter Terrace.

The corporate history of ASARCO is well documented. Accounts of expansion, strikes, and the jobs provided to the city of El Paso are only part of the story. Perhaps the best-known account is *Smeltertown: Making and Remembering a Southwest Border Community*, a detailed and excellent study by Monica Perales. She explains how, through the generations of men who worked for the company, a sense of company culture and loyalty was created. Perales also includes information about the women, but because her study starts with the company's creation, and because the American Smelting and Refining Company at first only hired men as smelter workers, the women's story is not highlighted—although she does present a thoroughgoing analysis of how her grandmother transitioned from a Mexican citizen to a US community activist.

It was the promise of steady employment and a new life that drew most of the grandparents and great-grandparents to Smeltertown. That is only one half of the equation; the other half is the role the women played in establishing homes and creating a community.

The family stories include connections to Pancho Villa as part of the history of the area. One woman we interviewed told us the story of how her Grandma Pepe, who was married at age thirteen, was so beautiful that Pancho Villa wanted her. The only reason he did not claim her was that her husband was one of his men.

The women who came to Smeltertown and created homes for their families did so in the shadow of the smelter. Although the buildings in El Alto are described as tenements, the women planted morning glories and other foliage to enhance the look of their living spaces. Across the highway, many of the adobe shacks rented by the families were transformed with household money, the families acquiring indoor plumbing and floors not made of earth. They did not earn any home equity or even reimbursement for their efforts, just the pride in making a comfortable home for their families.

ASARCO was known for paying higher wages compared to the rest of El Paso, but many women worked outside the home in skilled jobs, such as seamstresses at the Popular Department Store, to supplement the family income. For a time, young women could receive training in skilled jobs through a technical school for girls in Smeltertown. Young men could also obtain training through the YMCA on the grounds.

Women established small businesses, including informal lunchrooms that provided hot lunches for the men working in the smelter. Others opened restaurants, bars, and small convenience stores that became family businesses.

Abuelas, grandmothers brought from Mexico, helped care for the children, so extended families lived for several generations in Smeltertown. The story of Smeltertown is one of family and community that the women created through their church, the school, and their common experience in a small industrial city. The sense of community is so strong that even now, reunions are held every year in August in El Paso.

ASARCO established its El Paso, Texas, location in 1899. Accounts of domestic life as told by the women who lived in Smeltertown around that time are scant. In order to hear the stories of these women firsthand, our project begins with the 1940s, when World War II changed the role of women forever and some of the women worked in the smelter; through the social revolution of the 1960s, when conservative Hispanic mothers were trying to raise daughters with traditional family values during what is called the Sexual Revolution; and continues to 1972, when the houses of Smeltertown were torn down. The demolition was a result of a lawsuit by the city and state, which attested that the arsenic, lead, and zinc emitted by the smokestacks were dangerous to people's health, particularly the health of young children living in the area. Interestingly, a number of El Paso citizens opposed the destruction, seeing in the stacks historical significance and possible tourist interest. And cleanup has been time-consuming.

The spirit of the Smeltertown community is remarkable. They did not think of themselves as deprived. Letty Jaso recalls that she was "just happy, even though we didn't have running water. . . . I just recall being happy. . . . I had a good childhood." Her brother chimed in: "Same with me. I don't know if you could say we were poor, but if we were, we didn't know it because we were happy. I just remember running everywhere, to the river, church, around the school." When asked about the difficulties in raising a family in such small houses, their mother responded: "Really it wasn't, as long as you're happy. With my kids and my husband, that was all that mattered to me." Lily Gomez Patrick remembers that it was not until they moved out of Smeltertown that they realized they were poor and Mexican.

As the last generation of Smeltertown women and the children they raised age, it is important to chronicle their stories, particularly those of the women who were the heart of the community.

Our team consists of Marcia Hatfield Daudistel, author of a number of prizewinning books, such as *The People of the Big Bend,* published by UT Press, *Paso,* published by TCU Press; Mimi R. Gladstein, the books and co-editor of the American Book Award–winning *The Last Supper of Chicano Heroes: Collected Works of José Antonio Burciaga;* and Carol Eastman, among whose many photo and documentary exhibits is "Children of the Border: Juárez/El Paso," developed through a grant from the Texas Commission on the Arts. While Hatfield Daudistel and Gladstein interviewed women who lived in Smeltertown, Eastman photographed them. The interviewees shared their old photographs from the time when Smeltertown was their home, providing a contrast between then and now.

Because we wanted to provide a full picture of the women of Smeltertown, we also reached out to some of the daughters of fathers who were managers and supervisors and who lived in the Smelter Terrace part of El Alto. They have scattered far and wide, but some have been generous with their remembrances and photographs. Locating sources is a complex and engaging process.

Although there have been some publications about Smeltertown, the role of the women and their domestic and family life has been touched on only briefly since the emphasis usually has been on the corporation and the men who worked there. The stories of the women are a necessary component to complete the history of this unique community. We could not help but pass by the smelter towers and wonder about the women who made their lives there. The now middle-aged sons and daughters shared their memories about their mothers and grandmothers, and the mothers, aunts, and grandmothers who survive were very happy to share their experiences. Our fear that these stories would be lost as the years went by was a valid one, as two of our interviewees have passed away since our project began.

Marcia Hatfield Daudistel
Mimi R. Gladstein
Carol Eastman

Chapter One

Bienvenidos

In 1881, Robert Safford Towne came to El Paso. According to the *Handbook of Texas:*

> In 1887 the ambitious Towne went to Argentine, Kansas, where he secured the backing of the Kansas City Consolidated Smelting and Refining Company for the construction of a major smelter in El Paso to process lead and copper ores from mines in Mexico and in the American Southwest. Towne bought 1,156 acres along the Rio Grande for $3,757, and within five months the El Paso Smelter, with a 100-foot high chimney and a workforce of 250, was ready to begin processing the high-grade Mexican ore.[1]

According to the historical records of the American Smelting and Refining Company (ASARCO), the smelter became a part of ASARCO in 1889. Many workers came from the mines in Mexico to begin work at the El Paso facility.

From 1910–20 during the Mexican Revolution, many families fled north to El Paso. Dolores Romero remembers: "All my sisters were grown up when I was born; I was born when my mother was

Workers in early Smeltertown.
Courtesy of El Paso Public Library Border Heritage Collection.

forty-five, so my parents were refugees during the turmoil in Mexico, and they were told that they could stay here, but that they had to become citizens, but if they went back to Mexico they couldn't come back. My mother was a very old lady when she became a citizen."

Narcisco Jaso's parents came to El Paso in the early 1920s. "Pancho Villa loaded a lot of people, young and old, in a long train. They sent that train over to Juárez, old Mexico, away from the Revolution, and from there, everybody got out and came across the river here to El Paso," he said. "And that's how my parents got here. In those years there was a lot of work on the railroad building; some of the parents were hired right away and they were sent to Kansas to live out there so they could work with the railroad. Some people stayed in El Paso, and they got close to a plant that was called at that time American Smelting Refining Company, which is now ASARCO."

The Revolution was the deciding factor to leave Mexico for the family of Salvador "Chito" Sanchez. "My parents emigrated from Mexico. My mother was from Durango; my father was from Zacatecas. And my mother emigrated with my grandmother because her father was killed in Mexico," he said. "My grandmother and grandfather used to be pretty well off in Mexico, in Durango; they used to have a big ranch; they used to raise horses, and during the Revolution the Mexican military apparently came to the ranch and my understanding was that they wanted a particular stallion, a beautiful horse, and they pretty much wanted the horse without paying, and they forced my grandfather to lose that horse or else the family would be hurt. So what happened was they forced my grandfather to buck, to break the horse, and during this he was thrown off the horse and he hit the fence and he was killed. So my grandmother immigrated to the United States with about seven children at that time, and my mother was the second from the youngest." Salvador had three uncles, one that worked with the railroad, one at the Portland Cement

Company, and one at ASARCO. They all lived in Smeltertown. His mother met his father in Smeltertown, and Salvador, his four brothers, and two sisters were all born there. His father worked thirty-eight years for ASARCO.

Sisters Dora Luz Sanchez and Anita Zubia Lerma were born in Smeltertown. Their grandfather came from Monterrey, Mexico, and their grandmother, Esther E. Lopez, was born in El Paso. Their grandfather was working at ASARCO when he met their grandmother. "They had moved to Arizona where he was working at a plant over there in Arizona, and my mom was born over there in Arizona, my aunt Esther was born over there, and an uncle, Miguel, were born over there," Dora said. Their great-grandfather also worked at ASARCO.

Zubia family home in Smeltertown.
Courtesy of the Zubia Family Collection.

Carmen Frausto does not remember what brought her father to La Calavera, where she was raised, but her husband remembers how he came to live in Smeltertown. "No, I wasn't there. I was born in Juárez. My mom was born in California. My dad was born in Zacatecas, and they met and had us and [when] I was five years old . . . we came to live in El Paso, which is, we start out in smelter." His father did not work for ASARCO. "My dad had an aunt that raised him when he was born; we called her grandma. When my dad was born in Zacatecas, his mother died giving birth to my dad so they brought him over to live with his aunt in Smeltertown, and he was raised there until sixth grade. He was going to Courchesne School and finally his grandmother came from Zacatecas and took him back to Zacatecas, and that's where he lived until he was around twenty-two years old. His grandma died, so he came back to Juárez and that's where he met my mom. We were naturalized through my mom." Jose's father did not work at ASARCO, but worked in the moving and storage business and did odd jobs.

Carolyn Rhea Drapes's great-grandfather worked for ASARCO. "The family emigrated with the company; a lot of people were able to come to this country because ASARCO had smelting and refining locations throughout; I believe it started in South America and went north through Mexico and then crossed the border and the families came with it so you have pockets of people who came from specific villages or cities."

Even if the men of the family did not work at ASARCO, family members did, and the entire family would live in Smeltertown. Maria Caro Lopez's father came from Mexico and worked at El Paso Electric Company as a janitor. "At that time all the people without passports could come to the United States. The doors were open, so he was one of them that came, I don't know how, but he didn't understand English at all," she said.

Maria's mother also came from Mexico. "She brought three children: Amalia, Francisco, and Altagracia, a baby. That little girl was an angel; she died when she was nine years old." Maria's mother married her father after they met in El Paso. Her mother's house was close to where her father worked, but both sides of their families lived in Smeltertown. Maria married Alberto Lopez Senior, who went on to become the manager of the YMCA in Smeltertown.

Angelina Sarabia Rivers became one of fifteen children when her mother became stepmother to her husband's seven children, including a three-month-old baby, when his first wife died. Angelina's mother had eight children with her husband. They made their home in Buena Vista. "My father was transferred from the cement plant in Arizona to the cement plant on the outskirts of Smeltertown, where it still is. Not working, but still is. And then he settled in Buena Vista," she said. "My father and his brothers and mother were sent away from Mexico City where he was born . . . to Juárez because of the Mexican Revolution. My father was the only one that came across to the United States all the way to Arizona to work, and my grandmother and aunt and uncles stayed in Juárez."

Irene Rosales Santana was born in Smeltertown. Her parents and grandparents lived there after they emigrated from Durango, Mexico. "When they emigrated from Mexico they stayed there and they never moved. We would move from one house to another because everybody was renting," she said. Neighborhoods within Smeltertown formed not only because of extended family renting homes near one

Water delivery in early Smeltertown.
Courtesy of El Paso Public Library Border Heritage Collection.

Laundry day in early Smeltertown.
Courtesy of El Paso Public Library Border Heritage Collection.

another, but also based on the area of Mexico where they previously lived.

There were three or more generations of immigrants, predominantly from Mexico, who came to El Paso. They were escaping political unrest and diminished economic opportunity, and had the hope of a better life for themselves and their children. They believed the opportunities for more than subsistence wages were to be found at the railroad, the cement plant, and at the smelter. Their extended families came and lived in the area, so strong family and community ties were established. In addition, housing, although very primitive, was available at a low rent. They began their new lives with hope and established and raised their families in the shadow of the smelter. It was time to make a home.

Chapter Two

Making Our Homes

Within Smeltertown were a group of communities: Smelter Terrace, which included Smelter Hill; El Alto (the high); El Bajo (the low); and La Calavera (the skull). El Bajo was the largest section of Smeltertown. La Calavera was named for its location in Skull Canyon along the road to the Smeltertown Cemetery. Buena Vista and Flashlight, gone now and part of Pacific Park, were located outside of Smeltertown, but were populated by many families who had lived in Smeltertown.

Smelter Terrace and El Alto

The residents made clear distinctions among the areas within the land around the smelter. Smelter Terrace and nearby Smelter Hill were company-owned houses occupied by the families of upper and middle management. Elizabeth Woodside Welch, Peggy Walters, and Janet Nelson spent some, if not most, of their childhoods in Smelter Terrace. Originally, Smelter Terrace had six large, two-story houses provided by ASARCO for the families of upper management. When the railroad came through, only the large superintendent's home remained. New homes were built for the upper management families with large lawns and generous driveways.

Even lifelong residents of El Paso would have found it difficult to locate Smelter Terrace. After entering the entrance to the smelter and gaining admittance, a visitor had to proceed past offices, over railroad tracks, past smokestacks and blast furnaces to reach it.

According to Elizabeth Welch, "There before you was an oasis with a small lake, green fields and trees, and six houses. It was something like going from Kansas to Oz. Lifelong El Pasoans were always surprised to find it hidden away, although the smelter had been in existence since 1887."

It was separated from the rest of Smeltertown by elevation and economic circumstance. At one time a locked fence patrolled at night by a security guard also separated Smelter Terrace from El Alto. "The manager of the smelter, Ed Tittmann, and his family lived in the superintendent's house, built in the early 1900s. It was an elegant house with a brick courtyard, a coach house, maids' quarters, and a separate

Memorial World War II fallen heroes street names.
Courtesy of Special Collections, University of Texas at El Paso Library.

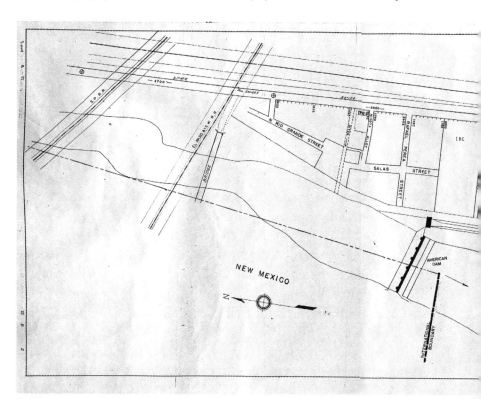

laundry building," Elizabeth remembers. "The other five homes were more modest bungalows. They were arranged in a circle separated by lawns and broad drives. Our house overlooked the Rio Grande and Mexico."

According to Monica Perales in her book *Smeltertown:*

> Besides the luxury of running water, electricity, and telephone connections, the residents of Smelter Terrace enjoyed summer boat rides and winter ice skating on the plant's cooling ponds, as well as the use of a company bowling alley, reading room, and tennis courts. For single men, the company provided a boardinghouse and dining hall, or they could find boarding in the home of a local family on nearby Smelter Hill.[2]

The other homes in Smelter Hill were there for a reason, Elizabeth said: "Since the smelter was built in horse and buggy days, the parent company, American Smelting and Refining Company, built houses adjacent to the smelter in order for employees to be on site in

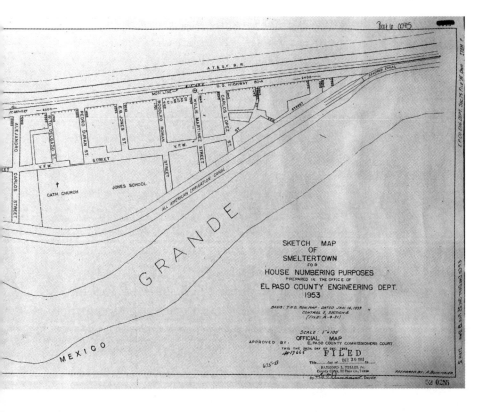

Smelter Terrace and lake.
Courtesy of Special Collections, University of Texas at El Paso Library.

the event of an emergency, such as a big house fire." Because these events did occur, the company had trained workers in fire fighting and had their own fire-fighting equipment. "I have memories of the smelter whistle going off in the middle of the night, the alarms sounding, and my father and the other men rushing off to direct the fire-fighting operation. Once the fire was so large, the tall hills behind the smelter glowed red in the reflection," Elizabeth added.

Elizabeth Woodside Welch and her sister, Nancy, and brother, John, were raised by their parents Lena and Tom. "My father . . . was the superintendent of the smelter, and I spent my childhood living in an enclave of six homes appropriately, if not grandly, named Smelter Terrace. It was a unique environment."

The wives and mothers of Smelter Terrace were educated women. Janet Nelson's mother earned a BA from the School of Mines, now the University of Texas at El Paso, in 1927. She never worked outside the home; however, she did maintain an active membership in a professional women's organization, AIME, the American Institute of Mining Engineers. "She was a homemaker, but it seemed a pretty easy job as we had inexpensive maids that came from Juárez Monday morning and returned Friday evening. The maid did cleaning and a little cooking," Janet said.

Not all the wives in Smelter Terrace were homemakers. Peggy Walters remembers that Bess Kelly, the wife of the plant manager, taught school, first at E. B. Jones, the school on the grounds of Smeltertown, and later at a school in El Paso. "I also remembered that my great aunt, Maybelle Adkins, worked as a secretary at ASARCO for many years."

They were a tightly knit group, brought together because of their husbands' careers at ASARCO. Lena Woodside and Margaret Nelson both had husbands who graduated from the College of Mines. Elizabeth remembers: "They were of varied backgrounds. My mother, Lena Woodside, grew up in Ysleta, where her widowed mother was

Nancy and Elizabeth Woodside. *Courtesy of Elizabeth Woodside Welch.*

Elizabeth, John, and Nancy Woodside.
Courtesy of Elizabeth Woodside Welch.

postmistress, and then moved into El Paso to go to El Paso High. Isabel Burt was Danish, plainspoken, and an excellent cook. My mother and Margaret Nelson were friends since their early married days. Mary Tittmann grew up in Salt Lake City and graduated from Brigham Young University. Catherine Cunningham had grown up in South Carolina and was a trained nurse. Betty Paul was younger than the rest of the women."

The women of Smelter Terrace isolated themselves from Smeltertown. "I never went to Smeltertown, and I assume my mother did not either. We children went to Mesita School via carpool. There was no interaction between the workers' and management's children, I am now ashamed to say," Peggy remembers. "We didn't seem to pay much attention to Smeltertown. I remember driving into Smeltertown once when my father needed to deliver something to one of his workmen."

"The women who lived in Smelter Terrace became good supportive friends not only because of proximity, but also because of common interests in the success of the company which employed their husbands," Elizabeth recalls. The women of Smelter Terrace socialized among themselves. They visited each other for coffee klatches, played bridge with friends from El Paso, and kept a collective maternal eye on the children. It was the era of 1950s family life idealized in television and books.

"My mother did some coffee klatches, especially with Mrs. Paul, who also lived on the Terrace. She liked to work in the yard with flowers. The smelter provided lawn mowing. She read *Fortune Magazine* faithfully and other finance magazines as well. When my father got home from work, they would sit in the backyard with a 'highball' and discuss the market and which stocks to buy or sell."

Janet, Peggy, and Elizabeth all have happy memories of growing up in Smelter Terrace. "My life as a child on the Terrace was great. Smelter was such a great place to play, with lots of open space to explore and run around. Every afternoon in summer we swam in the lake [pond used for metal refinery]. I used to love to go through the trellis entrance to the Terrace near the train tracks to mill through a pile of scrap metal parts that the smelter would melt down. I think that's what the pile was for," Janet recalls.

"It was a wonderful place to live when I was a young girl," Peggy said. "We had a large grass field—we called it our football field— alongside of the manager's house. We swam in the lake that was there—I now wonder about what was in that water. We did have to have a typhoid shot each year—we got that at the company medical office in the plant."

None of the children of Smelter Terrace attended Courchesne Elementary, located a mile away, or to high school at E. B. Jones, but went to Mesita Elementary School, then El Paso High, both located close to the university. Transportation to school at Mesita Elementary and El Paso High required a walk to catch the school bus, and then a second bus to go to El Paso High. Since Smelter Terrace was remote from the rest of El Paso, it was difficult to socialize outside of school. "I wanted to play more with my Mesita school friends, but it was quite a jaunt to drive there, and so I didn't get to as often as I wanted," Janet remembers. Peggy remembers being relieved that her family moved to town when she was fourteen, an age when socializing was very important to her.

"Since carpooling their children to school in El Paso or running errands in town was a twenty- to thirty-minute drive, the husbands walked to work at the smelter offices, leaving the women with the family car, needed to drive out of Smelter Terrace to accomplish their traditional tasks of carpooling to the elementary school—first Dudley, which was torn down, and later Mesita Elementary, grocery shopping, and errand running," said Elizabeth. Some of the men returned home for lunch, since office buildings were located around the cooling ponds nearby. The mothers also spent a lot of time driving their children to piano lessons or into town for movies and visits with their classmates. "We had to cross several sets of railroad tracks to drive out of Smelter Terrace, and we always allowed time to wait for a train. Train sounds were a big part of my childhood. Ore was brought in and dumped in piles, and refined products shipped out. At night the empty cars were shuffled around the tracks, and I went to sleep with sounds of chugging engines and bumping railroad cars. I missed that comforting sound when I moved away," Elizabeth added.

Even though the teenagers of Smeltertown and Smelter Terrace attended El Paso High School together, there was very little interaction between them. "At El Paso High, I had to wait an hour for a second bus to pick us up as there were only two of us. The other girl lived not in Smeltertown but on the east side of the smelter railroad tracks, where there were more houses than on the Terrace. Can't remember what we called that area. We didn't seem to associate that much with them as they were a ways away, and I don't remember there were many kids there."

Smelter Terrace children were close friends and playmates because of their distance from their schoolmates in town. Elizabeth's sister, Nancy, and Ann Tittmann were the oldest; Margot and Julie Tittmann, Jack Nelson, Jim Burt, Larry Burt, Elizabeth's brother, John, Janet Nelson, and Peggy Paul were the neighborhood friends. "Over the time I was six to age twelve, there were eleven children with an age gap of six or seven years from the eldest to the youngest comprising our neighborhood playgroup. We all had two or three playmates close in age. It was indeed a village, and all the mothers kept an eye on all the children. There were four boys and seven girls and often our games and activities included everyone," Elizabeth remembers. "All summer we roamed free around our unique environment. We rode bikes, played tag football, Red Rover, or practiced track events such as broad jump and high jump on the grassy fields. The bookmobile visited every week, keeping us supplied with summer reading. We waited for our fathers to come home from work to convince one of them to take us swimming in the lake," Elizabeth said. This lake at one time was filled by water pumped from the Rio Grande, so the children were required to be inoculated for typhoid every year at the Smeltertown infirmary until the lake was pumped out and filled with water from a desert well. "We called the area where the water poured in the Bathtub, because it was always warm and a sandbar formed around it," Elizabeth continued. "This was a safe, shallow place where we all learned to swim under the watchful eyes of our parents. There was a diving board and stairs in the deeper part of the lake and a floating dock anchored in the center."

The Fourth of July was a neighborhood celebration since Smeltertown was outside the El Paso city limits, and fireworks were legal. Lena Woodside gave an annual party, inviting not only the neighbors but friends from El Paso. "When it grew dark, the fathers would supervise lighting the sparklers, pinwheels, Roman candles, and finally the skyrockets. It was a fun, communal time, as was the experience of growing up on Smelter Terrace," Elizabeth said.

"I remember great Fourth of July celebrations with all the Terrace families. They went together and bought large amount of fireworks," Janet said.

El Alto

Just across a low wooden fence separating the management from the workers were company-owned apartments, described by Monica Perales in her book *Smeltertown* as "tenement-style row apartments made of adobe bricks and hollow concrete blocks." Most of these homes were small, primitive adobe dwellings with dirt floors; many lacked windows. These apartments lacked indoor plumbing, gas, or electricity. Two communal bathrooms, one for women and one for men, were provided for the residents. The apartments were very small, one or two rooms, and making a home in such limited space was very challenging. The workers of El Alto also had access to water provided by the company, but this water had to be hauled to the apartments by the residents. Despite these privations, the

Smeltertown family on front porch.
Courtesy of Special Collections, University of Texas at El Paso Library.

residents set about making these apartments their homes. They made great efforts to improve the appearance of their small homes by planting flowers for beauty and vegetable gardens to stretch food money, which was frequently spent in the company store.

Irene Rosales Santana would climb to El Alto to deliver the lunches her mother prepared for the workers when she was a child. She remembers the church and the apartments.

Alicia Sarmiento Ramirez's grandmother lived in El Alto. "I thought to myself, I wonder why they live up there. I noticed it was like in Chihuahuita; it smelled. Like the bathrooms were outside." Her family lived in El Bajo and had indoor plumbing with a cesspool. "My grandmother's apartment was two bedrooms and a little bitty living room and kitchen, with the bathrooms and showers outside," she added.

Luis Jimenez remembers the church that burned down, and that El Alto was "a little village that was on top of ASARCO." "After the church burnt down, then the people were told they had to move," said Angelina Sarabia Rivers. "My brother said he remembered that there was a tunnel in El Alto into ASARCO."

Carmen Rosales Frausto's mother was born in El Alto. "My grandfather lived at La Calavera, so when they told her to move from

El Alto, my mom went to live with him." Her mother also attended a vocational school there; Carmen thinks it may have been coeducational. "I think it was for both, but since she was in homemaking, that was only for girls. I have a picture of her when she was at the school when she was twelve years old."

The families we interviewed have few memories of El Alto, just that it existed and there was a church located there on the western side of Smelter Hill. Some remember the bandstand built by ASARCO in El Alto and the social life that revolved around the church. The church, known as Santa Rosalia, burned down on March 11, 1946. Then ASARCO reclaimed the land for plant operations and demolished the small homes.

La Calavera and El Bajo

The homes and land in La Calavera, the Skull, were located in Skull Canyon and adjacent to the Smeltertown Cemetery. El Bajo was the largest section of Smeltertown and was located on the banks of the Rio Grande. The land and the structures in both areas were owned by individual landlords. The employees coming to live in these areas were drawn by their proximity to the smelter, while those who did not work for ASARCO came to live among extended family.

The houses were frequently little more than a few adobe walls, a primitive roof, and dirt floors. The vast majority of the homes had no indoor plumbing. It was up to the tenants to make any improvements that would make their families comfortable. These rented homes were vastly improved, added onto, and in many cases were hooked up to main sewer and electrical lines. The tenants were free to improve these properties however they wished. They left behind transformed homes when they moved, but had no equity in them.

The homes located in La Calavera were on larger pieces of land than those in El Bajo, which allowed tenants to keep chickens, cows, and horses. Gardens had more space and were more prolific because of the access to water.

Dolores Romero, a former El Paso community activist, lived in La Calavera and remembers Skull Canyon: "I have five sisters, and like I said, we used to have all kinds of food around; we had chickens; we had fresh eggs; we had rabbits. And Skull Canyon was a beautiful place. It had different fauna and flora, but when Executive Drive [came in], they knocked down everything. And as a matter of fact, the water used to come from Mesa Street. There were hardly any buildings when I was small. The water used to go through La Calavera, a big arroyo, then it would go into the Rio Grande. And it was a beautiful place. We used to go up the mountains and have a lot of fun."

Dolores described their home without indoor plumbing, but with an outhouse. Water was bought and hauled to the house in containers. She remembers that some houses in Smeltertown had water, but were not connected to sewer lines. She became a community activist at the age of fifteen and left Smeltertown, but returned. "Where I used to live in La Calavera, there never was any plumbing until Jonathon Rogers was elected mayor [1981–1989]; that's when they put in water and the sewer line. I also helped run his campaign, and he was a good friend."

Across from La Calavera is the Smeltertown Cemetery, where Raquel Alva Sanchez's family members are buried. "That was ASARCO, the old part where the cemetery is, and all that is left is the new burials where my mother, father, grandfather, and uncle are buried. They left the east side of the cemetery, but the new part, as you go in ASARCO, people went and put American flags and there is a gate

Old La Calavera.
Courtesy of El Paso Public Library Border Heritage Collection.

Smeltertown Cemetery, 2017. *Photo by Carol Eastman.*

and all is evened out."

When Raquel was asked where the bodies were in the oldest part of the cemetery, she was told they were still there, but the markers and headstones were leveled. "My mother died only fourteen years ago, fifteen in December, and she was determined to be buried in the Smelter Cemetery, with my father, with her mother, and with her father and brothers. I think her brother was plotted down. There was a lot of built-in cement, granite, and crosses, and they just got all that flattened down," Raquel said.

Marta Sanchez Marquez has relatives there. "Both of my father's parents are there, one of his sisters and brothers are there. One of the graves is not marked."

Jose Luis Frausto went to the cemetery. "I can see the crosses from the freeway. They die and there is no one left to take care of them. My wife's grandma is there, and I went over and did some cement work with some gravel and took a generator and made her a tombstone." Carmen explains which graves are not marked: "It must have been the first ones buried, that is why the tombstones are all broken, since their relatives are already old, there was no one to fix them."

Carmen Rosales Frausto was born in La Calavera, where her family lived with her grandfather. "We used to have real nice memories over there because we were a very united family and we used to have a lot of fun."

Carmen and her husband, Jose Luis, met in La Calavera. "I used to hang around with her brother a lot and I knew her sister," Jose Luis said. "One of her younger sisters was dating a friend of mine, so they got together and said, 'Let's invite him for a blind date and let's go to La Calavera.' I went then and I met my wife."

Social life for the young people centered around home and the neighborhood. Jose described where they went for their dates: "We walked to the river. Everybody would hang around on the black bridge on the river, underneath it. It was the hiding place for everybody. We used to walk there and then go back to her house in La Calavera."

Most of these houses were not torn down in 1972, as were the others in El Bajo and Smelter Terrace. Now La Calavera consists of a few older houses, and the residents have lived there for most of their

Home in La Calavera today. *Photo by Carol Eastman.*

Black Bridge over Smeltertown.
Courtesy of Special Collections, University of Texas at El Paso Library.

lives. When families moved, an elderly family member would often decide to stay in the home they had lived in for decades. Ruben Escandon's grandparents came to La Calavera, and he still has a cousin who lives there. "He just stayed there forever, he's the only one that stayed there."

"I went riding around there the other day," said Ismael Holguin. "There are houses there, but the houses had at the most two bedrooms. It would be a two bedroom and kitchen and dining or something like that, but it was maybe half [the size] of [my] house. People would leave." Today, La Calavera appears nearly deserted; the few people there are surviving, but are mostly elderly and cling to their former community.

El Bajo

A pedestrian bridge separated El Alto from El Bajo, another area of land not owned by ASARCO, but by individual landowners who rented the land at a nominal price. Workers were able to build their homes on these plots of land and were free to improve them. These houses were on unpaved roads, and were named by the letters of the alphabet until they were renamed in honor of veterans of World

War II: Rafael Pereas, Willie Barraza, Alejandro Carlos, Rito Delga-
do, Pedro Duran, Rodolfo Romo, Willie Martinez, and Carlos Lopez. Ramiro Escandon remembers that while the residents owned
some of these homes, "A lot of [the residents] had landlords. I don't
know who the landlords were, but some of the [tenants] bought their
homes. They lived there forever until they tore them down." Ellen
Ramsey, who taught school at E. B. Jones for many years, remembers
the adobe structures. "It was acceptable, it wasn't pretty, no. But it
was people's yards. They were pretty because Mexican families care
about their surroundings and their gardens. You saw them all water-
ing the streets and gardening. There were still dirt roads there."

The childhood memories of the children who lived in El Bajo
were happy ones, revolving around their large extended families and
the activities at their own school, E. B. Jones, and the church. None
of our people interviewed remembered experiencing any jealousy of
the children of Smelter Terrace. Several commented they didn't know
they were supposed to be poor because everyone was the same.

It was not required that residents renting land and building or
renting houses be employed at the smelter, so many family and extended family members came to live in houses close to their families. The parents of Ramiro Escandon, both from Durango, Mexico,
met in Smeltertown and married. Ismael Holguin, now a resident of
Buena Vista, was born in Smeltertown in 1933 and remembers that
most of the residents of El Alto and El Bajo came from Chihuahua,
Mexico, as did his parents, who came from Camargo, Chihuahua,
Mexico.

Carolyn Rhea Drapes lived in El Paso, but was a frequent visitor to Smeltertown because her mother's twelve siblings were born
there. Carolyn points out on a map where her grandparents and extended family lived. "So if this is east, their house would have been
over here," she said. "The house was here, the outhouse was here;
then they added on these little row-house rooms, I think four, so this
part of the house had one bedroom, a kitchen, and a living room.
And then next to it down this way was a laundry room, so they had
running water and they had gas 'cause they had a gas stove. So the
kitchen was over here. But my mother said it burnt twice."

When Carolyn spent the night with her aunt and uncle and

cousins, she was surrounded by extended family. "I tell people this: you had a porch, you had the living room, you had one gigantic bedroom, a kitchen, and the bathroom. My aunt and uncle and five children were in one bedroom."

Household chores, laundry, and cooking kept these homemakers busy. Since many of the families lived within a sort of family compound, the women in Smeltertown who worked outside the home relied on grandmothers and aunts to watch the children. The laundry room in Carolyn's grandmother's house was used for two families, with the aunts who did not work outside the home doing the laundry and helping her grandmother with the cooking. The families in Smeltertown benefitted from the presence of extended family members. It was a communal effort to raise children, make homes, and be successful.

Raquel Alva Sanchez's mother was born and raised in Smeltertown and lived there all her life. "The only thing she always told us is that she was raised very poor, in a one-bedroom house, and it was cold and she had to sit behind the wood-burning stove where my grandmother would cook. She learned to embroider and to crochet behind that stove; she never went to school, but with books she taught herself. She could speak and write very good English. I don't think there was a school."

"I was born in 1930 in Smeltertown, and I still remember her very young. We lived by the river in a two-bedroom house; it was all three of [the children] and one that died in between my oldest sister and my brother. He died of pneumonia. So we were actually four, and he died so we were only three, and we ended up being nine," Raquel remembers. Raquel's father began working for ASARCO that year after working as a caddy at the El Paso Country Club.

After her family moved away from the river, they relocated to El Bajo, where her mother began improving the home they moved into. "My mother had a lot of pride. When we moved to that house on Doniphan, the first things she did was put in the bathroom, put in butane gas in the house, the water heater, and build the wash room with the washer and dryer."

The renters were free to add on to whatever sorts of residences would accommodate their families. The residents, in many cases, put in the water lines at their own expense to connect a home to the main lines on the road. In one small section of El Bajo, electricity was installed, and more sections followed. Ramiro Escandon remembers a typical home in Smeltertown from his childhood: "The houses at Smeltertown were all mostly there already, I was trying to think of the traditional home . . . the size of the family [determined] how many beds you had, but you walk into the front room, a small front room type thing with a little sofa and chairs, and then to the right was a door. The next door would be the bedroom or if it was a pretty large home, there might be two bedrooms, but you'd still go right through to the end of the house and the very last room usually would be the kitchen." Frequently, the women found employment outside the home to help provide the improvements to their homes for the comfort of their families, although here, too, renters' improvements would not earn them equity.

Eighty-six-year-old Doris Lozano and her husband, Narcisco, raised their family in El Bajo. Narcisco remembers his grandparent's house in Smeltertown: "All of the houses were made from adobe; the only thing that separated one family from the other was an adobe wall, so you could hear noise right and left from the other houses." She also recalls that the rent for the plot of land was as little as $3 a month. "Everybody built their own houses, I guess they started building something from cardboard, but then they started building the houses with adobe. In those years they called them *paracaidistas,* which means parachutist, because they would just drop down on the piece of land."

When Dolores married in 1956, she and her husband, Narcisco, made their home in Smeltertown, as well. "I moved with my husband when we got married, and we lived there for so many years, and it was nice and quiet. The kids grew up there, all the people were very friendly. I never had any problem with anybody," she said. In her new neighborhood, she was surrounded by her family. "My sister-in-law used to be there. I guess she was my best friend. My brother-in-law's wife used to live there, too, with her kids. We had a lot of fun. She used to go to my house, make food for everybody, get together."

Dolores's daughter, Letty Jaso Borunda, describes El Bajo: "It was like a small community; we had cousins and aunts and uncles

Above, from left,
Letty Jaso Borunda,
George Jasso, Paul
Jaso, Dolores Lozano
Jaso, 2015.
*Photo by Carol
Eastman.*

Left, clockwise from
bottom, Letty Jaso
Borunda, Narcisco
Jaso, Paul Jaso,
George Lozano
Jasso, and Dolores
Lozano Jaso, 2015.
*Photo by Carol
Eastman.*

living there, so everybody knew everybody, until people started moving out of there."

The Jaso family moved into a house with four rooms and no indoor plumbing, only an outhouse, but it was eventually wired for electricity. "In the living room we had a bed, one bed. I think my Mom and Dad slept in that one. In the next room were two beds, and that's where my brothers and I, all three of us, slept," Letty added. Letty, her brothers Paul Jaso and George Lozano Jasso (who retains the original spelling of their last name), along with their parents, left Smeltertown when Paul was five and Letty was nine. The rumors of the smelter closure caused many families to find homes elsewhere. "There was a lot of panic because that was their home, they didn't know where to live, that's all they knew," said Letty.

Although Letty, Paul, and George were children when they moved out of El Bajo, they remember the house they lived in. "This house had four rooms from what I remember. It had the kitchen and then you would go into the living room, and then there was a small bedroom where you could fit one bed, and there was another room, I guess where the boiler went; that's all that was there. Where the boiler was, it wasn't so much like a regular floor, it was like bricks, cement. Everything was in the back of the house, so the kitchen was in the back of the house. It was very, very small. We did not have a bathroom, we had an outhouse."

George remembers an improvement his father made on the house. "I remember my dad had purchased a washing machine for my mother. He had made a back room also so we could shower; there was cement and [because] he is a very intelligent man, he had made a shower, and there wasn't hot water, but we enjoyed it in the summer time. We would heat the water in the winter so we could take baths."

George Jasso remembers the rumor that the smelter was emitting toxic lead. "Even back then we had been there when they started building, we had seen [the smokestacks] going up layer by layer. That is what I understood for why we had to leave," he said. The Jaso family moved to the northeast side of El Paso when they were given notice their home was to be torn down.

Letty shares her reflections on her childhood in El Bajo: "I recall most I was just happy, even though we didn't have running water, we didn't have a big house, we didn't have a lot of extra stuff that kids have nowadays. I just recall being happy, I was very content with what I had, never wished I had what somebody else had. I was

Buena Vista Park, 2015. *Photo by Carol Eastman.*

content with my life, I was very serene, I had a good childhood."

Buena Vista

The small community of Buena Vista was across the highway, but in spite of the distance, the residents still felt a part of Smeltertown. This was an upwardly mobile move for the families since the land was bought and owned, not rented. Ramiro Escandon's mother was originally from Smeltertown, but the family moved to Buena Vista in the 1940s, when Ramiro was born, and they stayed. His mother was a traditional homemaker, and his father worked for ASARCO for thirty-eight years, from the age of sixteen.

Ismael Holguin's family originally lived in El Bajo, but eventually moved up to Buena Vista. He remembers the owner of the land. "I think the lots cost about a hundred dollars at that time, fifty feet wide by 250 feet, and they bought them and they could pay a dollar a week or something," When Ismael came home in 1956 after military service in the Navy, he and his wife moved to Buena Vista. "We lived with Mom because the house was about three or four bedrooms, real huge, the living room was maybe half of this house, so we lived there. In about four years, I saved money. My brother found out they were selling this land," Ismael said. He had just recently landed a job with Richard Azar, the owner of Dickshire, the Coors distributorship. Then Ismael's brother told him of an opportunity in Buena Vista. "He told me 'Hey, brother, they're selling that lot over there, mijo, and I wish I could buy it. I don't have the money. Why don't you ask your boss if he could lend you the money and buy it?' Six hundred dollars was a lot of money at the time, because I used to make $55 a week." His employer, Richard Azar, advanced Ismael the $600 needed to buy the land, deducting a small amount from his weekly salary until it was paid off.

Luis and Leonore Jimenez are part of a large extended family living in Buena Vista. Luis was born and raised in Buena Vista, and his brothers and his mother were still there when he came home from Vietnam in 1969. His wife Leonore came to live in Buena Vista in 1971, when she and Luis married. "This house belonged to Mom and Dad," Luis explained. "I was the baby of the family. My mom

Vietnam sign and trumpet at home of Luis Jimenz, 2015.
Photo by Carol Eastman.

Home in Lower Buena Vista, 2016. *Photo by Carol Eastman.*

and dad told me I was born on this property here. My mom and dad owned the house over there. They owned this house, too, but my mom passed away as they were building it, and my brothers, we helped build the house here. I had stakes here so I was the one who stayed."

"This is family to us," said Leonore. "All of us are here in the houses lived in by Luis's family." Luis's uncle, Ismael Holguin, lives across the street.

The move to Buena Vista was regarded as a vast improvement over living in Smeltertown. "I know we were better off then. The houses in Smeltertown were back to back, wall to wall," Luis said. "The front yard was from about here to there, the backyards, not too much. We had a backyard. I remember there was a little water running 'cause from the sinks in the kitchens, people would run a hose and wash dishes and a little stream would run through the street into the river."

Originally, Buena Vista had an upper section on top of a hill and a section below. Most of the homes in the lower section are gone, bought from the homeowners and torn down to make way for highway construction. Blasa Mendoza Marquez and her husband, Carlos,

Home in Upper Buena Vista, 2016. *Photo by Carol Eastman.*

moved from Buena Vista because of the construction.

Blasa was born in Buena Vista, and her father worked for the Southwestern Irrigated Cotton Growers Association. Her husband Carlos is from El Bajo. They met at Santa Teresita Catholic Church in Buena Vista. When they married, they built their home there. Now they live in the Upper Valley of El Paso. "We live [in the Upper Valley] because they took all our homes away," said Blasa. "We had been there forever. He built our home. When we were engaged he bought a piece of land, bought some adobes and built us a home." Carlos remembers that the thirty families who would be affected took action. "We put up a fight; we hired a lawyer. Thirty families got together and hired Arditti." Carlos feels that the families got a better price for their homes by doing this.

Alicia Sarmiento Ramirez was also born in Buena Vista. "My dad and my grandfather worked at ASARCO, so my dad bought land in Buena Vista . . . two parts, down on the bottom and up on the hill. That's what brought us there." Alicia did not feel there was any feeling that the residents of Buena Vista were somehow economically above the residents of Smeltertown because they owned their land. "We figured we were the same. The thing was that when we went from this little school over here, the elementary school, and then we had to go to Jones School, which is in Smeltertown, we were petrified because they said that that was where the gangs were. But it was not so, it was because there were older people living there than us," Alicia said. "When we went to school in Buena Vista, we looked at each other because we didn't even know that Anglos existed. We were always in the, as you would call the barrio, you know right there in Buena Vista, so the teachers were talking to us and it was like, 'What is she saying?' So if we asked each other [in Spanish], we'd get the ruler, you're supposed to speak English. Well we didn't know how to speak English. So we either learned or we died. My husband says 'You don't have an accent like some of the people,' and I say, 'Well, we had to learn it or we died!' "

Angelina Sarabia Rivers has a brother, Gonzalo, who still lives in Buena Vista in their parents' home. Although many of the residents have family members who worked at ASARCO or lived in Smeltertown, Angelina recalled that "Most of the workers that lived in Buena Vista did not work in ASARCO. The workers in Buena Vista worked at the cement plant, at the cotton gin which was right next door, a very few at ASARCO, and maybe one or two families at Peyton."

Angelina's father worked at the cement plant. "My father was transferred from the cement plant in Arizona to the cement plant in the outskirts of Smeltertown, where it still is. Not working but still is. And then he settled in Buena Vista." She points to a map to show us where her house was at the lower section of Buena Vista. "There were three grocery stores: the Alvas, the Lopez, and the Flores, and the Lopez also had a bar." She points out where two gas stations were located. "The freeway goes where the church used to be; it took the back of our house. . . . This used to be our front lawn. Our front lawn used to be a hundred feet long."

Today, Buena Vista shows pride of ownership and tradition. The residents are a tightly knit community with an active Catholic Church, Santa Teresita. The homes are immaculately kept, and the yards are well maintained. There is a small park in Buena Vista that is one of the cleanest and best kept in El Paso.

Frausto front yard, Pacific Park, 2016. *Photo by Carol Eastman.*

Flashlight and Pacific Park

In an area now known as Pacific Park, there is a group of homes that were once in the neighborhood of Flashlight, which no longer exists. Flashlight is now part of Pacific Park. In this area, land could be purchased so the residents would become homeowners. The small development has an active Catholic church—Saint Jude's—where activities bring the residents together. Dora Luz Sanchez lives in Pacific Park with her husband. "When we got married, we were living down the street, but then my husband built this house. This is Pacific. Flashlight was on the other side, in Rio Road and El Vida. This was desert. There used to be a drive-in here called the Texan, right in this area. That was many years ago. And then they started building this neighborhood. That's when we moved from Smelter to this neighborhood, Pacific Park, with my grandma and my aunts and all my uncles."

Carmen Rosales Frausto and her husband, Jose Luis, live in Pacific Park. "When they decided to tear it [Smeltertown] down, we moved here." They live down the street from St. Jude's Church and have lived in this quiet, well-maintained neighborhood for many years.

Marta Sanchez Marquez's family was one of the first families in the area. "My father moved here to Pacific Park after he built his house in 1951. He was one of the first ones. We lived in the part called the Flashlight area, on the other side of Pacific [Street]." She was raised in Pacific Park with her five brothers. "Most of them, at one time, lived here in the Pacific Park area. I live just up the street. I never grew up in Smeltertown, but my three oldest brothers were there in their early childhood." She attended first to sixth grade at Zach White Elementary School, then to E. B. Jones for her last year.

She met her husband, Victor, in the neighborhood. "My husband worked at ASARCO twenty-eight years. He was raised in Smeltertown. When we got married, we lived with his father and two brothers for a year and then we bought a home, but after seven or eight years, we moved here. My father had property here, several pieces of land, so we built our house. We have been here since 1979."

As is the case in Buena Vista, Pacific Park is also a neighborhood of extended families, making their homes in close proximity to one another. Pride of ownership is apparent here, as well, with the homes built by the families themselves.

Chapter Three

In and Out of the Kitchen

There is a German expression that identifies the domain of women as being "kinder, kuchen, kirsch," that is children, cooking, and church. That would certainly seem to apply to the women of Smeltertown, except that many of the women learned skills that not only took them out of the kitchen but led them to jobs away from Smeltertown. When asked about women working outside the home, Ramiro Escandon remembers that "Most of the women, and in my memories, my Mom . . . the women were home. They were home people. They didn't work." Ellen Ramsey, who taught school in Smeltertown, also remembers the women as being mostly stay-at-home moms. "I don't recall any of the women that worked in ASARCO. My feelings about the women in Smeltertown was that since the smelter opened, the men had jobs that paid enough to support the family so the women didn't have to work. And for people like me, in those days we could have someone from Juárez come clean for $18 a week."

"They didn't work," indicates a common attitude that defines only that done away from the home and for pay as work. For the women of Smeltertown, however, the kitchen was not only a domain for family nourishment, it provided an opportunity for the women to use their skills to earn money. Art Alva remembers that his mother prepared lunches for the teachers at the E. B. Jones School. In the morning he would take orders, then return home to place them and return them to the school. He says that he usually had about eight orders. It was not unusual for him to go home at noon, as most students went home to have lunch. His mother charged thirty-five cents for a lunch of tacos and enchiladas. Anyone who has shared memories with family members knows that sometimes events are remembered differently. An experiment by the UTEP Psychology Department illustrated that even eyewitnesses who see the same event from different angles can remember it differently from one another. As Raquel Alva Sanchez remembers it, her mother would cook for the teachers at E. B. Jones School, who would put in their orders on Friday for tacos, enchiladas, gorditas, or caldillo—whatever they wanted to eat. Then the janitor from the school, whose last name she remembers as Claudio, would pick up the food and take it to the school and bring the payment. Raquel did not remember how much her mother charged. In addition, her mother served workers from ASARCO who would come to the house and sit at a big table she had there.

Other interviewees remember similar arrangements. Carolyn Rhea Drapes recalls that during her visits to her grandmother in Smeltertown, men who worked at ASARCO would "come down and walk across the street and have lunch at my grandmother's and there would be easily a couple of seatings . . . so they were paying for their lunches." And her aunt Maria's cooking skills were such that she was able to work for the El Paso Independent School District as a cook at E. B. Jones school once her youngest daughter Marta started attending that school.

Businesses associated with food were a natural evolution for women. Ismael Holguin said his mother had something like a neighborhood grocery store. He recounts that she also raised chickens, rabbits, turkeys, and ducks, and since at the time "there were no grocery stores for meat, the people would come and buy the chicken."

Since the store closed during the Depression, he was too young to remember it, except for what his mother told him about it. She explained to him that a major problem was that people would ask for credit, and when she questioned them about the fact that they were leaving for California, they would promise to send the money, which they never did. Her frugality and business sense, however, allowed her to save enough to move out of El Bajo in Smeltertown and buy a lot in Buena Vista, on which her sons built a house. Ismael and his wife lived with her when they first married. Ismael's mother began working when she was a child of seven. Her parents would send her out to wash clothes. Another memory shared by the Jaso family is of a woman who sold candy from her home. They remembered that when they got coins that were thrown to the children at baptisms, they would run straight to that house and buy candy. "It was like a big table, and we would go around and pick out what we wanted."

Food-associated businesses were a natural type of enterprise for women, grocery stores and restaurants chief among them. Salvadore "Chito" Sanchez remembers that his grandmother owned and operated a grocery store in Smeltertown. He recalls that it was "close to the bridge that goes across the river to the brick company. . . . It was small. She used to sell, no fresh meat, but other than that canned goods, soda pop, cigarettes, and milk." The name was Victory Grocery Store. "There were quite a few stores in Smeltertown. . . . Victory Grocery was one of the stores and there were, let me see, about one, two, three, four, five, there were about five grocery stores and one cooperative, they used to call one a cooperative, they used to sell bulk stuff I guess to the other stores and to the public. We used to call it the cooperativa." Irene Rosales Santana told of her grandmother's food-earning skills: "My grandmother, my father's mother, that I lived more with her than with my mother. I had to go in the morning and go to where they mix the mais, the molino, and they would mix the masa. And then from the masa I would come and help them do the tortillas, the corn tortillas." This was done at her grandmother's house, and Irene remembers delivering them all over the area. Her grandmother had "orders all around" and was able to make money that way.

The women of Smeltertown also earned money by doing

laundry for other people. Since there were four brothers and four sisters in the household of Blasa Mendoza Marquez when she was a girl, there were plenty of hands to help. The four sisters would get up early to help with the washing and would hang the clothes on the line to dry before leaving for school. The brothers worked around at the small farms by the river in Buena Vista. They also picked cotton, as did the girls. During World War II, some rural schools had what was jokingly called "cotton-pickin' vacation." Since the men were away in the army, the students, male and female, picked the cotton. When the cotton was ready to be harvested, the schools in small rural communities would close so the students could go into the fields. Las Cruces, New Mexico, had such a "vacation."

Although the majority of the women from Smeltertown families did not work outside the home, there were a number who did. Some used their domestic skills to work for prominent El Paso families. In his autobiography, Tom Lea writes of Pomposa Macías, who "had been washwoman, assistant cook, and everything for my mother."[3] When his mother died, Pomposa stayed on to take care of his little brother Dick. Pomposa was well-known in Smeltertown because of the status of the family she worked for. Lea's father had been mayor of El Paso at a time when thousands of refugees, some of whom settled in Smeltertown, poured into El Paso. The story goes that Pancho Villa and Lea Sr. had some conflict, after which Villa put a price on Lea Sr.'s head and threatened to kidnap his sons.

Carolyn Rhea Drapes's great-aunt Juana, who never married, worked for two of the four Kelly sisters their entire lives. The Kelly sisters were prominent in El Paso for many reasons: their father had been mayor and was significant in the history of the area, as he had persuaded President Taft to send additional armed forces to El Paso during the Mexican Revolution. Juana worked for Anne and Elizabeth Kelly, one who taught math at El Paso High and the other who was a librarian at the El Paso Public Library. As they never married, they continued to live in the family house. Their sister Mary married Howard Quinn, a geology professor who taught for many years at the College of Mines, which later became Texas Western College, and then the University of Texas at El Paso. Professor Quinn is identified as the object of one of the greatest pranks ever played in UTEP history. The story goes that one midnight, a group students lifted a sleeping 400-pound alligator from the pond that was its home in San Jacinto Plaza. The alligator was deposited in Dr. Quinn's office in what was then the Geology Building, but is now named Quinn Hall. When he opened his office and found the alligator, Dr. Quinn called out to his wife, who also taught at the college, "Mary, come look what I got." The occasion was documented by an *El Paso Herald Post* photographer. Another sister, Charlee, rose to the rank of a Lieutenant Colonel in the WACS, which was as high a rank as a woman could achieve in those days. Carolyn explained that her aunt also helped the Kelly sisters with their needlework for the altar society at St. Patrick's Cathedral. Together they maintained and sewed altar cloths, and she proudly displayed a "double wedding ring patchwork quilt sewed by the Kelly sisters" and her aunt that Carolyn inherited. In addition, she remembers that the Kelly sisters would hire her to rake leaves in the fall.

Other women from Smeltertown worked in El Paso. Madelaine Carrillo Gubanski spoke of her best friend's mother, who worked for Chris Fox. Fox, known as Mr. El Paso, was quite prominent in his day, having been sheriff and a major officer at the State National Bank. Raquel Alva Sanchez remembers her mother as "a woman with a lot of pride." During the Depression, her mother worked, washing and ironing for the people who owned Price's Dairy.

Another significant venue for employment for some of the women of Smeltertown was the Popular Dry Goods Company, known as La Popular by many of the Smeltertown inhabitants. Art Alva tells of his mother using the sewing and needlepoint skills she learned at the Smelter Vocational School to work at the Popular as a seamstress. Although it closed in 1995, for much of the twentieth century, the Popular was the largest department store in El Paso. Older generations of El Pasoans have fond memories of the store. It was a favorite venue for bridal registries and had extraordinary customer service. It provided jobs for many of the girls and women who learned sewing at the Smelter Vocational School and at the YMCA sewing classes. The Popular had a renowned design and construct department under the stewardship of Miss Effie Day. Generations of El Paso women had their wedding and bridesmaids' gowns designed by Miss Day.

A Miss Day dress was so distinctive that an *El Paso Times* news story tells of two El Paso girls at a West Point Ball recognizing that they both were from El Paso because of their dresses. In addition to dresses for everyone from the bride to the flower girls for weddings, Miss Day fashioned dresses for high school proms and the Sun Carnival Court queens and duchesses. Jobs were also available in the alteration department for men's, women's, and children's clothing. All of these created a lot of sewing jobs for graduates of the YMCA sewing classes and the Smelter Vocational School. The pamphlet created for the dedication ceremony of the Smelter Vocational School Memorial, which was held on Sunday, October 12, 1975, includes photos of women in the last graduating class of May 1939 and pictures of girls in various sewing and homemaking classes, including one photo of girls in a class with the caption noting that "each girl made her own dress."

Rami Escandon remembers that his mother worked at the Popular, among other jobs. At first she did not drive and got around mostly by bus. Later in life, she learned to drive, and in his words "drove her little Volkswagen" on her Avon route. She became the Avon lady for Buena Vista, Smeltertown, and Pacific Park. Hortex, a clothing manufacturing company owned by the Horwitz family, was another place where women who sewed could find employment. Dolores Lozano Jaso remembers working for the Horwitz family in their home and then in the factory, where she wasn't a seamstress but worked in quality control. She remembers Henry Horwitz fondly, recalling that he used to call her "Chiquita" and that he attended her wedding Mass.

Some of the women began working early, for various employers. At the tender age of fifteen, Blasa Mendoza (now Marquez) went to work for Kress, on the corner of Oregon and Mills Streets. Kress was part of a national chain of dime stores. As a stock girl she unloaded merchandise from delivery trucks and stocked it on store shelves. She explained, "At the time all the men were gone, and we did all the work that they used to do." She stayed on that job until she was about nineteen years old, and then went to work for Davis Hardware and Lumber as a bookkeeper. She had learned that skill at night school at El Paso Tech. It was when she was working for Davis that she met her husband.

Other outlets of national chains employed women from Smeltertown. Cecilia Flores Marquez's mother worked for J.C. Penney for eleven years. Dora Luz Sanchez worked at Farah, the pants manufacturer, before she got married, claiming that "everybody in El Paso worked at Farah." Some women who worked did a variety of jobs. Dolores Romero remembers her mother working in the cotton fields as well as sometimes doing housework.

World War II was the impetus for many women to begin working outside of the home. Blasa Mendoza Márquez spoke of her cousin Carmen Vera Martinez, who worked at the smelter. When asked about the type of work the women did there, Blasa recalls that they did "everything." She thinks they pulled the metals out of the cars and cleaned them. Alicia Sarmiento Ramirez recalls that her mother was basically a homemaker, but that she did go to work for a short time at ASARCO during the war, when so many men had been drafted—although her husband, who failed the physical because of his hearing, still worked at ASARCO during that time. Displaying a picture of a group, Alicia said "Everybody that's in that picture—they were making bullet casings."

Sisters Dora Luz Sanchez and Anita Zubia Lerma spoke of their aunt, Esther Lopez, who worked for ASARCO for forty-five years. Noteworthy is the fact that this Aunt Esther, who never married, started at the smelter when she was only fourteen years old. She lied about her age in order to get the job. According to her nieces, she worked those forty-five years without missing a day. Their mother also worked at the smelter during the war, but only for a short time, between one and two years. She left her son with a grandmother in order to be able to do so. Julietta Rojas quotes Enriqueta Beard's praise of the women she saw working at the smelter. "Se veian bellas!" she exclaimed. Rojas also quotes Priscilliana Torres, who explained that the work at the smelter was better than some of the domestic work women had been doing. Torres claims that they were paid the same wages the men had been paid ("nos pagan como les pagaban a los hombres"). Whereas Rosie the Riveter is an icon of how American women helped with the war effort and took over the jobs men left, one could say that El Paso had Susana the Smelterer, the symbol for the women who went to work for ASARCO during WWII.

Sometimes working outside the home brought problems that caused women to quit their jobs. Dolores Jaso explained that she had to stop working at Hortex after she married. As she recounts the story, they had a young girl working for them. One day, although she had left food on the table for the girl to give the children, Dolores returned home early to find no food on the table and her son without clothes. She did not want to tell her husband because the girl was pregnant by a married man, but when he found out, he told Dolores, "You're not going to work anymore." Alicia Sarmiento Ramirez remembers a similar story. When her children were very young she stopped working because the maid she had tending them called her and said that her year-and-a-half old son was in a tub by himself. Alicia did not return to work until her children were more self-sufficient. Then she worked in a variety of positions, including clerk and secretary, at schools such as Zach White and Morehead.

Sitting in the home of Connie Carrillo to speak with her and her sister-in-law Madelaine Carrillo Gubanski, we were shown the counter that used to be in Carrillo's Confectionary. Madelaine

Counter at Carrillo's Café, Smeltertown.
Courtesy of the Carrillo Family Collection.

Carrillo's Café. *Courtesy of the Carrillo Family Collection.*

explained that the men working at the smelter would "run" to have lunch because they only had a thirty- to forty- minute break. Their confectionary was closest to the smelter, and her mother would have a "luncheon special." She remembers that there was "always some kind of meat with chili and, of course, the beans and rice never failed." Sometimes there were enchiladas, tacos, stew, or soup.

One of the most storied businesses of the Smeltertown area, one that remains operative to this day, is Rosa's Cantina. Robert "Beto" Zubia and his wife Anita Lopez Zubia were owners of the cantina for many years. Their daughter Anita Zubia Lerma remembers her mother as the cook of the business. The Zubias owned the cantina for fifty-four years and sold it some six or seven years before our interview with Anita. Ismael Holguin also remembers that his wife used to work at Rosa's. Stories of the place abound. Anita Zubia tells of their receiving letters from German tourists advising that they would be coming on a certain date to climb Mount Cristo Rey and eat at

Rosa's. They requested that her mother make tacos like she made for them every year. As she recalls it, many people would put in their orders before the climb and then come to the cantina afterwards. Edna Gunderson, who was an *El Paso Times* reporter before she went on to be a key entertainment writer for *USA Today,* explains that Robert Zubia was "born in the ghost town of Smelter, a miniscule nest of impoverished workers driven away by ASARCO's emissions." This cantina was made famous by the Marty Robbins hit song, "El Paso." The words, known by most El Paso residents, tell of the singer's falling in love with a Mexican girl named Felina, whose whirling to the music at Rosa's Cantina inflamed the senses of the young cowboy. The words then go on to tell of a scene right out of a Hollywood Western. Although he rides away, ultimately he is drawn back by his love and ends up dying in her arms. Although Robbins denied that the song had any autobiographical source—some even argue whether or not he ever entered the cantina—local legend is strong, and when Robbins died, there were those who thought there should be some memorial service at Rosa's Cantina. Though the original owners are gone, the restaurant still merits attention every so often in articles about historic bars of the Southwest. In a 2013 review in "Dining Out," Adriana Chavez, the *El Paso Times* writer, put the cantina in the "recommended" category for its good service and decent food. More recently the famous landmark is encountering trouble similar to that of a number of the areas occupied by the people of Smeltertown. That is, a government group—be it the city (as in the case of El Bajo), the State (which razed part of Buena Vista to make way for a highway), or in this case, the Texas Department of Transportation—intends to take over part of the property. TxDot wants the property for a retention pond, to service a new elevated highway that is being built as part of the $600 million Border West Expressway project. The owners of Rosa's Cantina, Patricia and Oscar Lopez, are resisting because they need the lot for overflow parking and worry that limited parking will hurt business. (The original owner's son is married to one of Oscar Lopez's aunts.)

There are also other long-standing restaurants connected to Smeltertown. A short distance south on the Rio Grande, located on the site of what was once Hart's Mill and thought to be where Juan

Rosa's Cantina, 2016. *Photo by Carol Eastman.*

de Oñate crossed the Rio Grande on his way north along the Camino Real, is what once was a residence and then a stagecoach inn. According to Fred Morales, that property was purchased by Mrs. Virginia Mendez and her daughter and son-in-law, Mr. and Mrs. Alfonso Lopez. It was they who gave it the name "Hacienda." It has fed and entertained area residents for decades. According to local lore, the family was originally from Smeltertown.

Many of the residents remember with relish the exceptional cooking skills of grandmothers, mothers, and aunts. Of course, a mainstay of those memories is of the making of tortillas. There were many assertions of champion tortilla makers in the various families. Of course, there were also a few who remember a different culinary situation. "My mom, bless her heart, was not a very good cook" is the recollection of Alicia Ramirez. "We didn't starve," she said, but there was still the fact that she would cook meat until it was tough, and in fact, they would buy Poncho's chicken for their Thanksgiving meal. The tortilla, while it has a very positive image and is mostly remembered in happy memories, could also be used as a warning. When the family got a wringer washer, she was warned about getting her fingers

Zubia family tamalada. *Courtesy of the Zubia Family Collection.*

into the wringer. The result would be "a tortilla hand."

Other foods stirred good memories. According to George Jaso, his grandmother made "the best beans and red chile." Dolores Jaso remembers cooking sopa, or, in her words, "sopita" and beans. Beans were an everyday basic. Interestingly enough for this rather traditional community, not all the cooking was done by women. Cecilia Flores Marquez remembers that it was her father who taught her how to cook, as her mother was usually working during the day and he worked various shifts. Then she was given the responsibility of cooking for her brothers. She learned to make such staples as beef stew, beans and rice, and chili verde, her favorite. Her mother did cook on Sundays, usually making caldo de res. Cecilia's cooking skills stood her in good stead, because many years after the demolition of Smeltertown she opened a restaurant in the area of Artcraft Road, close to Doniphan Drive. The restaurant was open from 1987 to 1994; after her husband died, she had to close it because of insurance costs.

The exceptional cooking skills of the women of Smeltertown and their daughters and granddaughters is a tradition that continues today. Just as women in many parts of the Southwest follow the custom of making tamales in preparation for the Christmas season, so the "tamalada" is alive and well in the environs of Smeltertown. This multigenerational and multifamily ritual is practiced in much of the

Spanish-speaking world. Though ingredients may vary—in Venezuela, for example, banana leaves are used instead of corn husks—the basic outline persists. The name for this delicacy in Venezuela is "hallacas." Some groups even use avocado leaves. Fillings of chicken with a red or green sauce are not unusual. A hunter friend once gifted us with wild turkey tamales.

Dora Luz Sanchez was gracious enough to invite our team to a tamalada at her home. Following tradition, others in her family were part of the ritual. Her daughter Brenda Tinedo was there, as were her sister Anita Zubia Lerma, her niece Belinda Lerma, and her aunt, Rosa Maria Reyes. All the ingredients had been prepared before we got there, but we were able to assist in spreading the masa on the corn husks, handing them to keepers of the traditional filling of pork in red chile sauce, and assisting in filling the husks in preparation for steaming. The expectation was that over a hundred dozen tamales would be made.

Just as in many other Western cultures where women are limited to raising children, cooking, and church activities, so there were some men in Smeltertown who ascribed to that idea. Alicia Sarmiento Ramirez remembers her husband being angered by her request that he help out. "You know that's your job, to cook, that's your job," he reminded her, although he would end up helping and he was, according to her, "a very good cook."

The women of Smeltertown pursued a number of what were then considered the traditional paths for men, but not for women. Although many women of the time married right out of high school, a few did not; if they went on to college it might be to pursue what was humorously termed an "MRS" degree, since in college they might encounter men with better earning potential. Higher education for women was not a priority in most families of the time. Irene Santana had a different perspective. She counseled her children, the girls as well as the boy: "You have to have an education so you can be something." Her oldest daughter graduated from UTEP and works for UTEP marketing, and her youngest daughter has a PhD in microbiology and in engineering. Irene explained that her daughter got the degree in engineering to show the older men in the department who had deprecated her knowledge.

As of this interview, Carolyn Rhea Drapes is a lecturer in technical writing and rhetoric at the University of Texas at El Paso. When she completes her graduate studies she will have earned the title of Doctor of Philosophy.

Politics was another venue of interest to a few of the women of Smeltertown. Dolores Romero, who identifies herself as an "activist," became one when she moved back to El Paso after spending time in other parts of Texas, including Corpus Christi, San Antonio, and Refugio. Her experiences in Refugio, in particular, led to her commitment as an activist. There she learned that at the time, Hispanics could not eat in the restaurant inside the bus terminal. They had to take their food outside. She saw a sign in Corpus Christi that read "No Mexicans or dogs allowed." She also recalls reading that "the same thing happened to the Jewish people . . . way back in New York areas," when similar signs stated, "No Jews or dogs allowed." Dolores worked for equitable treatment for all people, not just Hispanics.

Dolores Romero, 2016. *Photo by Carol Eastman.*

Connie Carrillo and Madelaine Gubanski, 2016. *Photo by Carol Eastman.*

Alicia Sarmiento Ramirez, 2015. *Photo by Carol Eastman.*

Maria Cano Lopez and her son, Beto Lopez, 2015.
Photo by Carol Eastman.

**Carmen Rosales
Frausto.**
*Photo by Carol
Eastman.*

Irene Rosales
Santana, 2016.
*Photo by Carol
Eastman.*

Lily Gomez Patrick, 2016. *Photo by Carol Eastman.*

Ismael Holguin, 2015. *Photo by Carol Eastman.*

Carolyn Rhea Drapes, 2015.
Photo by Carol Eastman.

Narcisco Jaso and Dolores Lozano Jaso, 2015. *Photo by Carol Eastman.*

Angelina Sarabia Rivers, 2016. *Photo by Carol Eastman.*

Salvador "Chito"
Sanchez, 2017.
*Photo by Carol
Eastman.*

Raquel Alva
Sanchez, 2014.
*Photo by Carol
Eastman.*

Esther "Tilly" Lopez, first woman chairperson, ASARCO 25 Year Club.
Courtesy of the Zubia Family Collection.

Chapter Four

Hard Times

Strikes were a fact of life in most major corporations. The issues that led to these strikes are well documented by labor historians. It is the impact on the women and children of the striking employees that does not form a part of the history of labor relations in Smeltertown. In the interviews for this book, we heard stories about life in Smeltertown during these disputes.

Since ASARCO established their smelter in the late 1800s, labor disputes over the years were practically inevitable. ASARCO workers in El Paso and at their other locations, although unorganized, went on strike in 1912 protesting their long hours and low wages. The next year brought longer working hours and cut wages. During the Depression, ASARCO workers became members of the Mine, Mill, and Smelter Workers Union, although World War II diminished the clout of the union.

According to the website, Their Mines, Our Stories: Work, Environment and Justice in ASARCO-Impacted Communities: "Although the El Paso labor situation went through similar transformations and shifts of union base, what's distinctive about the El Paso labor story is how ethnic divisions, tensions around immigrant workers, and the political significance of the border have all contributed to labor politics. Humberto Silex was a Nicaraguan-born labor activist who became a key figure in the ASARCO smelter labor struggle and a celebrated union organizer. Silex fought against the 'Mexican wage,' a discriminatory two-tier pay system. His effectiveness as a union leader in the MMSW through the 1930s and 40s led him to be targeted by the US Department of Justice and then systematically blacklisted by virtually all employers in the El Paso area."[4]

The MMSW was discredited politically and faced tough financial times. The United Steelworkers Union had been attempting since the 1950s to become the union representing the ASARCO workers. In 1967 the MMSW union became part of the United Steelworkers Union.

The memories of the strikes reflect the families' struggles during a time with limited or no household income. Remiro Escandon remembers: "Now they were into strikes when they finally got unionized at the smelter, and that was a big issue because they'd go on strike for higher wages of course, and it was a big thing because they'd be out of work for a long time and then they'd go back to work." Maria Cano Lopez and her son Alberto remember that the settlement could bring a positive change. "I think when the strike was settled, I think that's when they had enough money to move from Smeltertown.

"They were able to purchase property; every time there was a strike and then there was a settlement, they ended with a cash amount, and so when that happened then that was enough for a down payment. So my grandmother's family moved in roughly '53, '52, to 1116 E. Nevada, and on Nevada Street, that's where my father went."

Salvador Sanchez remembers when his father worked at ASARCO and there was a strike every few years. "Well, there was no money to be provided. To my knowledge ASARCO would not honor the request of the workers and there was a union, I remember there was a union that represented the workers of ASARCO, and the union always fought and apparently they must have got everything their way because ASARCO did get the workers back—but I was only a kid at that time."

Not everyone in Smeltertown went on strike, since many residents were not workers at the smelter. El Paso ASARCO was not an isolated company town; it was located barely within the US border

ASARCO strikers protesting.
Courtesy of Special Collections, University of Texas at El Paso Library.

in the largest US-Mexico border city. It was on the banks of the Rio Grande. Across that river was Mexico, the home country to many of the workers. Many of the residents of Smeltertown were employed by the railroad or the cement plant or were working as skilled carpenters and bricklayers, and they had no disruption in income when ASAR-CO employees were struggling. Extended families living in Smeltertown could rely on much-needed support from relatives not employed at the Smelter. Irene Rosales Santana's family was not directly affected by any of the strikes. "My grandfather was in the railroad. At first he was in the El Paso Brick and then he was in the railroad. And then my father, he was a caddy at Ft. Bliss and then he became a cook at a medical center." She does remember some of the impact on the families of the smelter workers: "At that time I think I remember that they wouldn't pay rent because they were on strike. And it wasn't so much rent; it was $75, or $100," she said.

Carmen Frausto's brother-in-law worked at ASARCO. "They went on strike. The last one was about nine months and they used to take turns picketing. They used to get paid a little bit of money to keep going, but not the full amount," she said.

The smelter workers whose wives worked outside the home brought home much-needed income, particularly during strikes. Raquel Alva Sanchez's mother worked at the Popular Department Store. "I remember there was a time when I was going to graduate from the eighth grade and you would wear a dress, and then the big strike came. My mother had already bought the material when she worked at The Popular, and she had a seamstress make a dress. That strike lasted a long time, and they were hurting. And the workers were telling my dad 'You don't care how long the strike is, your wife is working at The Popular and you have an income.' So my Dad told my mother: 'Today you stop working.' She said, 'Why do you have to listen to what they say?'"

"'I'm not going to be subject to ridicule with these people telling me that I don't care about the strike, I care, I'd rather be working, I have nine kids.'"

Strikers outside ASARCO Plant, 1976.
Courtesy of Special Collections, University of Texas at El Paso Library.

Strikers protesting lack of on-site medical equipment, 1978.
Courtesy of Special Collections, University of Texas at El Paso Library.

Raquel's mother did leave the job she loved and never returned to outside employment. "She just came home," said Raquel. After the strike was settled, the settlement lump sum payment was enough to make a down payment on a house in El Paso, but her parents continued to rent their home in Smeltertown. "They rented the house for eternity because my mother didn't want to leave Smelter, and she cried and she cried 'I'm not gonna leave, I'm gonna stay here till I die.'"

In the November 10, 2009, *United Steelworkers News,* author

Manny Armenta reported that nineteen union members were to finally receive their pension benefits after eight years of litigation. "Each of these former employees worked at the El Paso Smelter for over twenty years," said Bob LaVenture, USW District 12 Director. "They should have received these benefits eight years ago. It is unfortunate that it took so long, but we are glad that they will finally receive the pensions they were due."[5]

In February 1999, 350 employees were laid off while another 100 workers retired in the next two years. The union negotiated for early retirement benefits for the long-term employees laid off in June of 2001. What came into dispute was the date these early retirement benefits were to be measured, the last day worked or the June 2001 agreement. "Because of the passage of time, many of these former employees may have forgotten about this dispute," LaVenture said. "I am proud that the USW never gave up and continued to fight for their benefits. This is what unions are all about."[6]

Armenta states in his article, "Each of the eligible former retirees will receive a pension of approximately $800 per month, monthly supplement of $300 until age 62, and retiree health care benefits.

"On February 3, 2009, Asarco LLC announced that it would not reopen the El Paso smelter, ending several years of controversy over the restart of the facility and renewal of its air permits. Asarco filed for Chapter 11 bankruptcy protection on August 9, 2005."[7]

A strike is never only about the workers; it is about the women who were supportive during the strikes. It was a time of reduced financial circumstances and the necessity of finding creative ways to continue to feed a family. The women who made and served lunches to the workers no longer had their small income. The following tells the story of the human cost in a strike.

Award-winning journalist and author Bryan Woolley (1937–2015) began his journalism career at the *El Paso Times* while still a student at Texas Western College, now the University of Texas at El Paso, in the late 1950s. The following story, "Rosa," is from his last book, *The Wonderful Room,* published by Wings Press. It is the first reference in the newspaper that referred to the homes in Smeltertown as "adobe shacks." It was a human-interest story that showed the effects, even on young children, of a protracted strike.

Rosa

The union at the copper smelter down by the river went on an illegal strike. Union leaders called the walkout because of some internal political rivalry, and the rank-and-file workers had nothing to gain by its outcome. They were just out of work.

Many workers lived in the adobe slum between the smelter and the river, called Smeltertown. They were poor. They had wives and children. When some workers defied the union leaders and tried to go to work, picketers attacked their cars with rocks and clubs.

The following Sunday, a heavy rain was falling, a rare sight in El Paso. When I arrived for work, Engledow [Ed Engledow, his editor] was standing at an open window, watching the rain, smelling it. He said, "Come here, son."

I joined him at the window.

"Grab your camera and go see what's happening on the picket line," he said.

"In this?" I whined. "I'll get soaked! Nobody's going to picket in this!"

Engledow said, "Get your ass out there and don't come back 'til you've got the story."

I had my own car now, a two-tone green 1955 Ford Fairlane with white-sidewall tires. I loved it. I wasn't about to risk it among a mob of club-swinging strikers. I called a taxi.

The driver stopped in front of the smelter gate. A single picketer stood there, holding a sign. He wore a soggy serape and a big straw sombrero like the ones that tourists bought in Juárez. The rain had destroyed its shape, and its wide brim drooped around the man's thin face.

On the other side of the road, a dozen cars were parked in a row, facing the gate. Each car held three or four strikers.

"Wait for me," I told the cabdriver.

"No," he said. "Pay me."

He made a quick U-turn and was gone. I was in the middle of the road, holding my Speed Graphic, my notebook, and an Army-surplus bag of flashbulbs and film holders. Quickly, I was wet as the picketer.

I shot a picture of him. "What's this strike about?" I asked, trying to sound casual.

He said nothing. He stared past my face.

"How long have you been standing in this rain?"

No reply.

I had no way to get back to the *Times,* no way to call Engledow. So I stood in the road, trying to protect my camera with my drenched sports coat.

The driver in one of the cars across the road opened his door, got halfway out, and waved. He was motioning me toward him. He was burly and had a big mustache and wore a brown felt hat. He looked like Pancho Villa. Three men were in the car with him. I was scared, but I went to the car.

"Get out of the rain," the man said. He told the man in the front passenger seat to move to the back. I climbed in beside the driver. "What you doing out here?" he asked.

"I'm a reporter. From the *Times.*"

"Yeah, I figured. Because of the camera."

"My name is Bryan Woolley." I stuck out my hand. The driver shook it. "Rudy Gonzales," he said. He introduced the other three men. I shook hands with them all.

They started talking about the strike. They didn't like it. They couldn't feed their families. Their union bosses were no good. Slowly, I relaxed. These weren't thugs. No clubs were hidden under their seats. They were getting a raw deal, and it was hurting them. I wanted to take notes, but was afraid they would stop talking if I opened my notebook. I just listened. We had been sitting maybe half an hour, quietly talking, gazing through the rain-streaked windshield at the miserable picketer across the road, when Rudy told me about Rosa.

She was his daughter. She was nine years old, a beautiful girl. She was a victim of polio and wore steel braces on her legs. She had outgrown the braces and needed new ones, but Rudy didn't have the money to buy them. If the strike didn't end soon, who knew when he could save enough? His voice was full of love and sorrow.

I cleared my throat. "Rudy," I said quietly, "may I take a picture of Rosa?"

Rudy didn't answer. He started the car and steered it through the rain to Smeltertown, to one of the adobe shacks. We all got out. A face, Rudy's wife's, appeared behind the screen door. She opened it and invited us in.

Rosa was sitting in the sparsely furnished living room. She smiled big when she saw her father. She seemed to light up the room and the whole gloomy afternoon. Rudy lifted her from the chair, sat down and set her on his lap. Rudy's wife made us coffee. We talked.

Finally I asked, "May I take the picture?"

Rudy told his wife what I wanted. She didn't want to be in a picture, she said. She didn't like the way she was dressed.

I shot a picture of Rudy kneeling, buckling the braces on Rosa's legs. Rosa was smiling shyly into my lens.

Rudy and his companions gave me a ride to the *Times*. I wrote the story and developed the picture. Engledow put them in the middle of Page One.

Next afternoon, an anonymous caller told Engledow that if I returned to the picket line, something bad would happen to me. It didn't matter. Two days after the story ran, the smelter workers refused to picket anymore. In defiance of the union politicos, they went to work.

I end this little collection of memories with Rudy and Rosa because theirs was the best story I ever did for the *Times*. And it taught me the power of the word. It taught me that telling the truth in a newspaper can do more good than you expect.

Chapter Five

Food for the Spirit

Smeltertown is gone, but its spirit endures—much of it maintained by the Church. It would be very hard to overestimate the crucial role that the Church played in the lives of the people of Smeltertown, especially the lives of women. In what was originally a dissertation and then a published book, Monica Perales's thoroughly researched study of the community, *Smeltertown: Making and Remembering a Southwest Border Community*, the Catholic Church is presented as a key component in a number of areas. Early in the community's history, one such concern had to do with what she terms the group's worry about the loss of "Mexicanness." A number of the people were apprehensive that with their children going to American schools and adopting American customs, there would be a loss of language and culture. But the community's loyalty to their new country became evident with the advent of World War II, when many young men from Smeltertown joined the military, and the women of Smeltertown displayed their patriotism with Blue or Gold Stars in Smeltertown windows. The young men of the Smeltertown area were quick to answer their country's call to service. Ismael Holguin had two older brothers that served in the military during WWII. One of them, Roberto, was wounded twice and awarded two purple hearts. Though his brother Andres also served, he was never shipped overseas. Too young to serve in WWII, when he came of age, Ismael joined the Navy in 1952. Women also contributed to the war

Drawing of the first church in Smeltertown.
Courtesy of the El Paso Public Library Border Heritage Collection.

effort: Holguin remembers that while the men were away, women "picked up the slack." He recalls that during the war, two of his sisters worked at the cement plant near the smelter. After the war, streets that had originally been designated by letters were renamed in honor of those Smeltertown heroes who died in the war.

Originally, Santa Rosalia was the name of the church that served the residents of Smeltertown. It was built in 1891, and the name reflects the original homestead for many of the people who moved to the area. Initially on the grounds of the smelter, the building burned in 1946 and was rebuilt at a location in El Bajo and renamed San José del Rio Grande. Eventually the name was changed to San José de Cristo Rey. Early settlers remember how the parishioners built the

Santa Rosalia, the first church in Smeltertown.
Courtesy of the El Paso Museum of History.

Santa Rosalia Church after the fire. *Courtesy of Ismael Holguin.*

original church and how the women helped by using their aprons to carry sand to the men who then created the adobe bricks. When San Jose de Cristo Rey was torn down along with the rest of Smeltertown, many of the people in the vicinity joined Santa Teresita church in the Buena Vista area. It continues as one of the important religious sites for the Smeltertown community. Leonor Jimenez spoke of some of the social activities at the church, such as a Mother's Day brunch, when the men cook for the women. Then on Father's Day the women cook, gathering all the dads and giving them "pins and stuff." Leonor also spoke of menudo sales, where the women would cook and earn money to provide for the church. Her characterization is that "it's a big family, that's what it is."

Another current site for nourishment of the spirit is St. Jude's Church in the Pacific Park area. Carmen Rosales Frausto and José Luis Frausto, interviewed in their home across the street from this church, tell the story of how in 1973, after Smeltertown and the San Jose de Cristo Rey church were torn down, some parts of the church, particularly parts of the roof and floor, were moved to what was at first going to be Saint Jude's Catholic Center. But in 1980 the site became the St. Jude's Church when Bishop Reymundo Peña presided at the groundbreaking ceremony. The women's organization there was called Hijas de María. A strong sense of community and historical connection to San Jose de Cristo Rey emanates from both the Santa Teresita church in Buena Vista and St. Jude's in Pacific Park.

Although the original community that was key in its inception is long gone, the annual pilgrimage up the mountain to the famous Cristo Rey statue continues. It is a significant religious event. The enterprise is a lasting testament to the character and dedication of a community, and the story of the construction of the statue, a pride of the district and of the entire city, includes many contributions by the female members of the community. The location is significant, as it is at the intersection of three states and two countries. The mountain is technically in New Mexico, but the monument was envisioned and financed by El Paso, Texas, church fathers. Fr. Lourdes Costa, who was the parish priest from 1924 till the 1960s, ministered to the congregation through the time when the old San Jose de Cristo Rey church burned and was rebuilt in El Bajo, near the E. B. Jones Elementary School. It was he who first proposed a plan to build a monument on the top of Cerro de los Muleros (Mule Drivers Mountain), which was then officially renamed Sierra de Cristo Rey. Opinions differ as to the inspiration for this project. According to Fred Morales, in his book *Smeltertown,* he did it in response to a papal encyclical issued by Pope Pius XI. The encyclical encouraged Catholic churches worldwide to create monuments to commemorate the nineteenth Centennial of the Redemption of Jesus Christ. The Mount Cristo Rey website claims that Fra Costa looked out his window one day

Santa Teresita Church sign, Buena Vista, 2016. *Photo by Carol Eastman.*

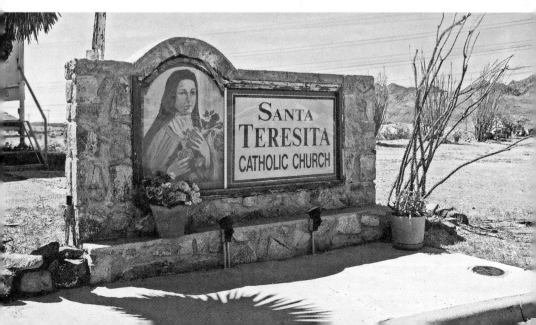

Exterior, above, and interior, below, of Capilla Saint Jude, Pacific Park.
Photos by Carol Eastman.

and "envisioned erecting a monument at the summit of this glorious mountain."

When Fra Costa proposed it, the Smeltertown congregation was enthusiastic about the idea, and the men and women contributed to the construction first of a wooden cross. Having received the concurrence of Bishop A. J. Schuler of El Paso, that cross was dedicated on February 13, 1934. Subsequently an iron cross made by the students of the Smelter Vocational School was installed. Then, in 1937, Fr. Costa got the idea to invite Urbici Soler to sculpt a major monument. That twenty-nine-foot limestone statue has served not only as a shrine and pilgrimage site, but also as a tourist attraction for the whole area. As the site was being built for the placement of the famous statue by Soler, women brought food and water to the men who were carrying sand and gravel to the mountain top. Prior to that, the official website for the monument states that men, women, and children had donated time and effort over a five-year period to help build the trail up the mountain as well as the foundation for the statue. Madelaine Carrillo Gubanski tells the story she heard of a friend's mother who carried buckets of rocks up the mountain during construction. Every account of the construction, which incorporated an arduous climb to the peak, includes testimony to the key role that women played in support of the men.

The monument was dedicated on October 29, 1939, and pilgrimages up the mountain continue to this day; the seventy-fifth anniversary climb was held in 2014. The one associated with Smelt-

Rebuilt church in Smeltertown.
Courtesy of the Buena Vista Neighborhood Association.

Urbici Soler carving the head of Christ, Mount Cristo Rey, ca. 1939.
Courtesy of Special Collections, University of Texas at El Paso Library.

ertown occurs on the last Sunday in October and celebrates the
Christian feast of Christ the King. Many Pilgrims also make the trek
on Good Friday. Many women join the men on the arduous climb
up the mountain. Newspaper accounts often quote the women who
are making and have made the climb every year. In his "Diamond
Jubilee" report, Ramón Rentería interviewed the Monarez sisters, Veronica and Maricarmen. They remember being rousted out of bed by
their mother once a year to make the climb, and they are encourag-

View of Mount Cristo Rey
from Upper Buena Vista.
Photo by Carol Eastman.

Statue of Christ on top
of Mount Cristo Rey.
*Courtesy of El Paso
Public Library Border
Heritage Collection.*

ing their children to preserve this tradition.

Veronica Monarez noted that she only missed one year, and that was because she was pregnant. Another newspaper story tells of one Julio Serrano, who decided to make the climb because his girlfriend, Rína Torres, and her family make the pilgrimage every year. One man who couldn't make the climb waited dutifully at the foot of the mountain while his wife did. The Jaso family now lives in far northeast El Paso, many miles from the smelter area, but they still make the pilgrimage once a year.

Not all climbs up Cristo Rey are for religious reasons. Irene Santana tells of climbing both for fun and with a group for a pilgrimage. The famous symphony conductor Leonard Bernstein used the leisure time he had before conducting the El Paso Symphony Orchestra to take a horse ride up the mountain and visit the famous statue. Carmen Rosales Frausto has made the climb many times. She recounts going with her son. Remembering the families who lost loved ones in World War II, Letty Jaso Borunda tells of a time when "all the people from Smeltertown went to Cristo Rey to thank God for bringing those who survived home and thanks that it was over." As Elena De Santos remembers the significance of this community effort, she points out that while most of what was once Smeltertown has been demolished—the homes, the smokestacks, the smelter—the "Christ of the Rockies" still stands. As she movingly puts it: "It stands as a testimony to the faith of those who built it."

Not every family participated in the annual pilgrimages or other faith-related climbs. Salvadore "Chito" Sanchez recalls that there was a certain group in the church that "did that kind of stuff," but he did not, nor did his "mom or my aunt, my sister, my mother's sister. We didn't like to go on the pilgrimage because it took too long to go with the procession up, but we did use to go to Cristo Rey and we used to go on our own, because at that time it was pretty much wide open and there was no vandalism and no gangs like there are now from across the border. But we used to go up quite a bit; in fact, we used to go with our BB guns, a whole bunch of us; we owned BB guns, and we used to go across the river on the bridge that went to the brick factory and then we used to continue along the railroad, follow the railroad, and we would end up in Anapra in Sunland Park

Letty Jaso's First Communion Day. *Courtesy of the Jaso Family Collection.*

and then we would go up to Cristo Rey." This, however, was a male outing, and no girls were included.

The community effort for the construction of the Cristo Rey monument was one of the more successful ways that Fr. Costa was able to inspire his community, to nourish their spirits. He was not always as successful at tamping down the rebellious spirits of his young female congregants, however. As it was with many members of the congregation, one of the Church's concerns was the issue of maintaining Mexican mores and culture. Fr. Costa would use his weekly newsletter, *Hoja Parroquial,* to address some of his apprehensions about issues such as chaperonage and dress. In Mexico, young women did not maneuver in public spaces without the accompaniment of an adult; young girls from Smeltertown's more traditional families were often not allowed to attend school functions because of the lack of chaperonage. However, Lily Gomez Patrick doesn't remember that as a problem; she recalls that the dances at school were chaperoned by the parents and attended by "everyone." During the flapper peri-

Dolores Lozano, right, and two friends.
Courtesy of the Jaso Family Collection.

od, the question of proper dress had even inspired Fr. Costa to write a poem titled "La Cristiana Coquetta" (The Coquettish Christian Woman) in which he took to task young women who adopted the short skirts and bobbed hair of the period. Although he did receive some negative feedback, he was undaunted and felt it his duty to preach proper behavior.

A number of the residents remember the church as a center for social activities—in particular, a monthly bazaar (kermes). Although she was not born till after the destruction of Smeltertown, Monica Perales remembers these kermeses as providing "a place where Esmeltianos shared memories."[8] Ramiro Escandon's family lived in Buena Vista and often went to these monthly events. He reminisced about the women being "very much into the church activities." They sang in the choir; they belonged to various church groups. They were also often part of the Church hierarchy in a number of ways. Felix Vazquez Jr. remembers that his aunt, who became a nun, had to learn to sing and play a musical instrument just as the priests did, and she began by playing the piano in the family home. His aunt and his mother learned from a woman who had been the Church organist for many years. Vasquez still marvels at this. "I don't know how she managed with fourteen children and still had time to go and practice. My mother, God bless her." His mother, Margarita Montoya de Vazquez, played the organ for thirty-five to forty years. The family lived very close to the church, and he recalls the story that the priest would come out and holler, "Margarita, Margarita! They're having a quinceañera. They just called and they are coming." Then his mother would go over to the church. Only a barbed wire separated the houses from Church property. It was only after she developed cancer that playing for the church became too arduous; her son remembers that she kept on playing at the house, however, when they got together on Sundays. His sisters were musical, as well, and all of them sang in the choir. He remembers one sister whose tone was so striking and her singing so beautiful that when she sang "Ave Maria" his "skin would get all tingly."

Carolyn Rhea Drapes recalls that her father spoke of how whenever he and her mother went to the church in Smeltertown after they were married, the people there would be excited to see her. "She had a really sweet voice and so they were all glad she was there because she'd sung in the choir and she'd sing with them." When Letty Jaso Borunda remembered that her mother Dolores Lozano Jaso used to sing in the Smeltertown Church choir, Dolores corrected her, saying

"I still am in the choir." In addition, since everyone knew everyone, they all congregated at the church, not only for services, but also for Bingo and carnivals. Lily Gomez Patrick explained that she could invite as many people as she wanted to her wedding, because her wedding was in the church.

One individual we interviewed was not Catholic like 98 percent of the people in Smeltertown. Madelaine Carrillo Gubanski recalls that for this reason she was not included in quinceañeras and other church events. Dolores Romero is another of the Smeltertown area citizens whose attitude toward the Catholic Church was not all positive. She recalls the Catholic priest talking about the devil a lot, and her fear as a child that if she looked out of the window, the devil would be there. Her attitude may also have been colored by the fact that though they were poor, her mother always saved money to give to the church. She told the story of wanting some money for an RC Cola, which her mother would not let her have because the money was for the "poor." The lessons her mother taught were from the Bible and encouraged helping others. "You always pick people up, you don't put them down," was something her mother continually repeated. Cecilia Flores Marquez's mother was also not active in the church and did not participate in the pilgrimages.

An interesting sidelight is that although there was not an official connection between the company (ASARCO) and the church, the company did contribute to the church in a number of ways. They provided monetary support, and during a number of years in the 1920s even donated funds to buy Christmas gifts for the children. These were distributed at the annual Christmas parties.

Nourishment for the spirit was often accompanied by nourishment for the body. One of the major contributions women made to the Church was by making food to sell, the funds then used to help buy needed supplies. Many of the stories about the Church have a culinary connection. Often, positive memories of community life are food-connected, particularly in terms of the church bazaars. George Lozano Jaso remembers that his grandmother, an excellent cook, would help the priest prepare the food; memory of the event still evokes happiness in him. Jaso, who left Smeltertown when he was twelve, remembers liking to go to baptisms at the church because they tossed coins there. He counts some of his fondest memories as being at the church during the holidays. "Culture shock" is the term he used for what it was like to leave Smeltertown.

Art Alva recalls that his family was very religious and that they all helped build the new church after the one on the ASARCO property burned down. His family also participated in building a house for the priest, his mother making gorditas to sell in order to help buy supplies for the construction. She would also wash and iron the altar linens.

Chopping onions and potatoes was a way that Blasa Marquez helped to get ready for a kermes. Her favorite foods at these events were red enchiladas, chicharrones, and chili verde. When Blasa and Carlos married in St. Teresita church, they provided mole for the whole neighborhood.

Raquel Sanchez remembered that Ruben Escandon's father would pick up her mother and take her to sell food to support the church. Like Art Alva's mother, Rachel's mother made gorditas to contribute to the building of the priest's house and washed and ironed altar linens for the church. Her family was very religious. Her Grandmother, who was a midwife, would lead the rosary after a home delivery. Rachel's mother and older sister would sometimes help in these deliveries. In her memoir, titled *Smeltertown, Texas,* Elena De Santos states that their life was "very much church centered." She explains that she used to help clean the church every week; an arduous job as there was constant dust emanating from the smelter. "The dust was quite disagreeable," she said, "—pungent, with a smell like arsenic, always excessively thick and penetrating every nook and corner."[9]

It is interesting to note that regardless of the negative environmental issues such as the sulfuric smells, the ash, and later the evidence of the lead contamination, the people of Smeltertown were not anxious to move out of the shadow of the smelter. Monica Perales notes that while "Esmeltianos argued that their children's health was important, so was preserving the place that had been their home for generations."[10] The *El Paso Times* quoted a woman resident explaining that she liked the people, the sense of community, the fact that one could leave the house unlocked because there was no fear of stealing. Sense of community was strong, and even though they were aware of the health hazards, the people were not willing to be thrust out of the place that had been home to some families for generations. This attraction/revulsion phenomenon was also evidenced in the reaction of many people in the El Paso area. El Pasoans remember the terrible beauty of the hot molten ore as it was poured onto the slag heaps. Robert Seltzer has called it a "hot orange river of steel."

Sometimes religious observance took place in both church and the home. Ismael Holguin remembers that his mother used to observe novenas. A novena is a prayer read for nine days, in this case to the Virgin of Guadalupe. After these nine days of prayer, his mother would give a dinner for all the people who attended. He recalls that she would buy a little pig and raise it, then pay someone to slaughter it, after which she would make tamales and other dishes from the pork. Holguin's home is rich with religious statuary and icons. He is particularly proud of a crucifix and a Virgin de Guadalupe made by an alcoholic artist whose story he recounted to us. Holguin's home, inside and out, is adorned with religious art. This was the case in many of the homes we visited. Statues of Madonnas and crucifixes hanging on the walls were common, and there were occasional altars, as well. Patios were adorned with representations of such saints as Our Lady of Lourdes, St. Joseph, St. Anne, and the Virgin of Guadalupe. Such statuary was clearly emblematic of the spirituality of the residents.

In addition to the more religiously oriented activities, the Church also sponsored sports teams. These included a women's baseball team run by the Catholic Youth Organization (CYO) that would play against teams from the area. The team was a mix of older and younger women and would play at E. B. Jones School at night.

While the Catholic Church was the major religious institution in the area, the YMCA (Young Men's Christian Association) was also an important factor in the community. Albeit of Protestant origin, the contemporary Y is open to all religions and races. And though it was ostensibly a male institution, it sponsored many social events that included girls and women. When it was first opened in Smeltertown, local Catholic officials were concerned that it would provide an alternative religious site for the residents, but that fear proved unfounded. The spirit that it nurtured was a social one as it showed movies, organized dances, and sponsored other cultural and social events. Young people gathered there to play checkers or dominoes. Maria Caro Lopez, whose husband Alberto Lopez Sr. ran the YMCA in Smeltertown, did not go to the church there, but to a church on Oregon Street in El Paso, Sacre Corazon de Jesus, the church she and Beto Sr. were married in. Maria Lopez remembers the Y as being a social center of Smeltertown, and her husband running the projector to show movies. Dances were also a big contribution to the social life. "They brought their strings, with their guitars," she remembers. She smiled as she told us how well liked she was because of the many good deeds performed by her husband, most of them women-centered: "'Beto, would you please take me to the hospital . . .' He always took all the ladies to the hospital." Alberto Lopez, who died in 2002 at the age of 90, was affectionately known in Smeltertown as "Beto de la Y."

Things spiritual did not begin and end with the Catholic Church and the YMCA. Many of the families brought with them superstitions and beliefs from Mexico. One such belief was in the powers of a *curandera*. Yolanda Leyva writes of the importance of such "skilled women," noting that this is testament to women's historical, if limited, power. This is also a case in which there is historical conflict with the Church. The Church often charged curanderas with sorcery and witchcraft. One popular curandera in the El Paso area had been denounced by a priest as having powers from the devil.

Curanderas are traditional healers, and their treatments vary with their particular abilities. Traditionally, *curanderismo* functions best in a community that has a shared system of beliefs. This was certainly true of the Esmeltianos. Some rely on herbs and natural medicine; others break and cast spells and rely on the faith of the individual being treated. Narcisco Jaso remembers when he was sick, lying on the dirt floor of their adobe home in Smeltertown as the curandera swept around him, chanting. He found the whole thing funny and began laughing, which brought a harsh response from his father. Elizabeth Holguin also remembers a harsh response when she laughed during one of the times her mother was "curing" her with an egg. Her mom "clopped" her with the egg. The egg looms large in the practice of curandismo. It is supposed to absorb the negativity from the individual who is suffering. One story that Yolanda Leyva recounts in her study "Healing the Borderlands Across the Centuries" is of the daughter-in-law of a curandera who discovers that the egg her mother-in-law had used in the healing process had "cooked during the healing." Irene Rosales Santana spoke of a curandera who believed that illness was sometimes the result of someone's curse. This woman would treat a high fever using an egg, which she would then break into water.

Sometimes Esmeltianos would go to Juárez to curanderas. Cecilia Marquez remembers that her mother frequented curanderas there and would take her children there; however, her father did not believe in them.

Besides the female curanderas (a feminine word in Spanish), Lily Gomez Patrick remembers that there was a man who lived in Calavera who did similar work. She says he was "kind of like a masseuse. He would fix your twisted ankles, your broken bones, your whatever." From her description it seems that he functioned similarly to a modern-day chiropractor.

In the Rosales family, everyone was delivered by a midwife. This was not unusual. Art Alva's grandmother was a midwife. His mother and his sister would help her deliver babies in people's homes. Dolores Romero is pretty sure she was born in La Calavera with the aid of a midwife. She also remembers that her grandmother was a midwife. Her husband's mother, a famous midwife, was also a curandera. For all her knowledge of herbs and curing and her other abilities, however, this curandera did not know how to read. "She would go into the desert on a horse with a little cart and pick up herbs, and she would take care of the people in the San Juan area." According to Dolores, her mother-in-law delivered Vikki Carr, the stage name for Florencia Bisenta de Casillas Martinez Cardona, the Grammy-winning popular singer from El Paso.

A situation might not call for a curandera, but much of a curandera's information about the healing powers of plants and herbs was part of a family's knowledge, often handed down through the generations. Madelaine Carrillo Gubanski remembers her family's beliefs in herbal medicine; they did not believe in medications as much as they did the traditional ways of handling women's issues such as childbirth and menstrual cramps. She tells of her mother binding her up with strips of sheets so that she would not lose her shape after giving birth; a certain herbal tea was brewed to handle menstrual cramps. Other families had different home remedies. Blasa Marquez tells of a time when her baby sister Teresa caught pneumonia at two months old. The family solution was to put her in the one room with a wood heater, pray all night, and give her herbed teas. Then, as Blasa tells it, "someone brought them a pint of whiskey" and told them to put a bit of it on the tip of the fingernail and feed it to the baby to relax her. They did so, and in the morning she was better. Today, many of the granddaughters find this belief in herbal and alternative medicine quite in keeping with contemporary values.

Stories of life in Smeltertown, whether it be in El Alto, El Bajo, La Calavera, or Buena Vista, resonate with remembrances of how the lives of the people were nourished spiritually by all of the religious and social activities of the Church. And while the YMCA and family traditions also contributed to sustaining the spirit, the Church was and is a bulwark of soul, and much activity continues around the two major churches in the areas where many of those associated with Smeltertown still live—Buena Vista and Pacific Park. Though she now lives in New York state, Angelina Sarabia Rivers still makes a quilt every year to be auctioned off at the Santa Teresita bazaar.

A booklet published to initiate a construction project for a new front entry, a new Sacristy, a meeting/classroom, kitchenette, and new rest rooms at Santa Teresita Church includes a history that highlights its original connection to San Jose de Cristo Rey in Smeltertown. Pictured inside are a number of the activities of women that support the construction fund. Among those is a garage sale, an enchilada dinner, a Mother's Day dance held at the Polly Harris Center, and a number of kermeses during the summer.

Chapter Six

Adios

The women of Smeltertown had grown up, gone to school, supported their church, and nourished and established families; they were emotionally invested in their community. Therefore it may not be insignificant that when the *New York Times* chose to write about the community response to the demolition of Smeltertown, they chose a woman and her granddaughter to picture in the story, headlined: "Polluted Town Doesn't Want to Move." In the photo Natalia Flores holds her two-year-old granddaughter, Melba Renteria, as the giant 828-foot smokestack towers over them like an ominous projectile. Writers from outside the area found it difficult to understand the feelings of the people of Smeltertown; after all, it had been shown that the area was toxic. One of the *El Paso Times* headlines notes "They Still Want to Call It Home." Juana Morales is quoted saying she is very happy to be living in Smeltertown, and Mrs. Catalino Alonzo attests that she has liked Smeltertown for all the twenty-six years she had lived there. *Fronterizo,* the Spanish-language newspaper from Juárez, also wrote about the phenomenon of resident resistance to leaving. In a March 1972 front-page story, they quote both José Seáñez and Manuel Medina, identified as officers of the Smeltertown Destruction Committee, a group that was question-

Empty land after ASARCO demolition, 2017. *Photo by Carol Eastman.*

ing the motivation for the move. Allen Pusey, the newspaper reporter, notes that even those who admit there is a pollution problem still don't want to leave. Why would that be? A variety of responses have been chronicled.

But before we say adios to Smeltertown, it is important to recount what led to the decision to move the citizens and demolish the community. A number of studies have covered the changing nature of the economy of El Paso during the decades following World War II. Many changes had already occurred before the final demolition. As the city grew, many Esmeltianos had chosen to move to newer residential areas. Parts of Smeltertown had already been demolished to make way for what was to become US Highway 85, a four-lane truck route. The YMCA had closed, as had a number of small businesses. At the same time, the whole country had become more cognizant of environmental issues. Then, in April of 1970, a suit was filed by the city of El Paso charging ASARCO with violation of the 1967 Air Safety Code. About a month later, the State of Texas joined in the suit against ASARCO. An important individual in amassing the evidence against ASARCO was Dr. Bernard F. Rosenblum, who at that time was the director of the El Paso City-County Health Department. Rosenblum and later Dr. Philip Landrigan, who was sent by the CDC, published a study in the *New England Journal of Medi-*

cine. In their study they indicated that fifty-three percent of the children who were living within the monitored area of the smelter had dangerous lead levels. The Esmeltianos were not convinced by the studies. A telling photograph of the time shows a sign painted by the citizens who were forced to move. It reads, "We don't like you Mayor Williams and Rosenblum."

Some theorize that what may have spurred city action leading to this move was not the lead, but the sulfur dioxide in the air. Students who went to Texas Western College complained continually about the taste of sulfur as they walked from class to class. Residents of the Kern Place area were also annoyed. Those who drove into town from the upper valley or westernmost areas of the city would see a yellow cloud sitting over the area as they descended from the higher mesa. But it turned out that the air pollution was not the only source of environmental danger. Once the city and county health officials began their investigations, much more was discovered. Not only was sulfur released into the air, but also lead, arsenic, and cadmium. According to contemporary reports, almost half the residents of the areas in close proximity to the smelter had lead levels in their blood above the acceptable limit. The children, in particular, were in danger because of the lead poisoning. A *New York Times* article reported that according to the United States Surgeon General, 102 out of the 416 children from Smeltertown had a count of over forty—the beginning level of abnormal. As Monica Perales later so poignantly put it: "The very industrial processes that had brought it life had destroyed Smeltertown."

Why had the citizens of the area not done anything about the situation? Arturo Islas, one of El Paso's pioneer Chicano writers, has one character in his novel *Migrant Souls* suggest an answer. Aunt Sally, who has moved to California and returns for a family wedding, attributes it to the lithium in the water. Islas, who grew up in Kern Place, a residential area that was continually plagued with the heavy sulfur in the air and where the lawns were often laden with lead, creates a scene in which Aunt Sally, an exasperated family member, questions the complacency of her relatives. She castigates them for accepting the status quo. Aunt Sally theorizes that the water department keeps putting lithium in the water so the residents will "stay nice and happy and obedient." In the 1970s there were a number of reports analyzing the tranquilizing effect of the high level of lithium in El Paso water. It was suggested as the cause of El Paso's low crime rate. Could it have contributed to the acceptance of the toxic situation in Smeltertown?

One of the women interviewed for this book remembers the beautiful roses her grandmother planted, and how they would become covered with black dust from the smelter. As she recalls it, her grandmother would casually shake off the black ash and return the rose to its original beauty. Another resident, even though he spoke about how bad the air was and how difficult it sometimes was to sleep at night, wanted ASARCO sued, but still did not want to move. Allen Pusey's articles highlight the fact that people had made many improvements on their houses and in some cases had actually built them—yet they did not own the land underneath them. Still many of these residents remained strongly attached to their community. Venturo Reyes, a seventy-two-year resident, spoke of wanting to spend his last years in Smeltertown, as did Rafael Rodriquez, who had called the area home for some fifty-two years.

Remains of second church in Smeltertown, 2017.
Photo by Carol Eastman.

Besides those who were forced to move out of Smeltertown, there were many residents who regretted leaving voluntarily in the years before all were forced to move. After her father had put a down payment on a house in central El Paso, Raquel Alva Sanchez recalls that her mother resisted moving. She remembers her mother crying and crying, saying, "I'm not gonna leave. I'm gonna stay here till I die." Marta Sanchez Marquez spoke of her grandfather, Yisdro Sanchez, who built a house in Smeltertown, and though he did not work for ASARCO or want his children to, he appreciated the very family-centered neighborhoods. He did not want to leave, and being forced to do so made him, in her words, "very ornery"—in fact remembered by everyone as being "a little grouchy."

Pusey notes that it was a woman, Hortencia Aguilar, who was the first person the city moved. She was a widow with six children, and two of them had been diagnosed with lead poisoning. The story emphasizes the fact that her living situation improved after she left Smeltertown, since she was moved into a two-story, three-bedroom duplex, next to an elementary school, with a convenient shopping area nearby. But many felt that their situation deteriorated from homeowner to renter when they left Smeltertown.

Access to public schools may have been a positive factor for Esmeltianos who did not resist the move. Students of high school age were used to catching the bus to El Paso High School, but the younger children were negatively affected when the El Paso Independent School District closed down E. B. Jones School. They then had to be bussed to Lincoln or Morehead elementary schools, some six or seven miles away. The E. B. Jones building had needed extensive work because of sewer problems, while at the same time the population of the school had declined. The building itself was sold for over $50,000 to be turned into a clothing factory.

A number of others have tried to clarify why the people of Smeltertown were so resistant to moving. Monica Perales, a key chronicler of the area, posits a number of explanations based on the importance of both family and community. Once the people were dispersed around town, she hypothesizes, the sense of "communidad"—which she sees as a word richer than the English equivalent "community"— would be lost. To many it was not just moving locations; the move encompassed a loss of values. To express the community's choice, a meeting was held on March 22, 1972, at the San Jose de Christo Rey Church, and the vote was overwhelming: the residents wanted to remain in their community and not be relocated. As noted, many of the residents did not see evidence of illness in themselves or their children. One Andres Bustillos, who had lived in Smeltertown for some fifty-four years and saw himself as healthy, attributed the concern with pollution to the inhabitants of the wealthier areas of town such as Kern Place and Coronado. He and other residents thought there was some reason other than the health of the children of Smeltertown that was behind this relocation effort, and even went to court to attest that no one in the community had died of lead poisoning. Notwithstanding their claims, in the coming year some two dozen families sought settlement with ASARCO due to high levels of lead in their blood. They reached settlement with ASARCO in late 1974.

In the end, no amount of resistance availed those who did not want to move. It was a choice between "move" or "be moved." By the end of 1972, Smeltertown was mostly deserted.

Though a number of former residents and some local historians have written about ASARCO, the smelter, and Smeltertown, interestingly it was a UTEP student in a history class paper who most strongly argues for the significance of the women. Julietta Rojas points out the fact that the residents called the community "La Esmelda," a feminine name. She challenged readers to look beyond the already amply chronicled perspectives of the company, and the Anglo and Mexican men. She underlined the importance of women in the building, creation, and survival of the community. For instance, she cites a female resident who was born and raised in Smeltertown and did not feel any health issues as a result. This woman also claimed that none of her twelve children had suffered deleterious effects, as the city health officials were claiming. Some women expressed concern not only about their move but about what would happen if they closed the Smelter. It had been a source of good jobs over the years. Rojas also quotes women who felt that the city had underhanded motives, wanting the citizens of Smeltertown to move because they had been building housing projects for low-income families, and they needed them filled. Emphasizing the feminine nature of the

The remains of Smeltertown, 2017. *Photo by Carol Eastman.*

resistance to leaving what had been home for so many, and for several generations, Rojas underscores that "La Esmelda" was a feminine presence.

The demolition of El Bajo was not the end. Today, when one visits the area where once a business thrived and many people lived, there is nothing. One by one all the institutions that sustained and nourished this unusual community vanished. E. B. Jones School was among the first to go.

With the destruction of the smokestacks, the last visible sign of the smelter is gone. Where there were once buildings, heaps of ash, bustle, and activity there is nothing. Only one building has not been demolished—and that in the hopes that it can be made into a museum of sorts. Where the homes—the adobe shacks as reported in news stories—the church, and the E. B. Jones School stood, there is nothing but grass, rock, and soil.

Still, echoes of the smelter and Smeltertown resound. Memories are stirred when one sees television stories about a contaminated city in Indiana, where what is termed the "smokestack effect" has toxic effect on the children of the nearby area. As in Smeltertown, residents were forced to leave an area of Gary, Indiana, called Cowboy Town. When one opens current local newspapers there are headline stories about future plans for the area, now that it has been "cleaned up." A June 19, 2016, *El Paso Inc.* story announces a pending sale of the ASARCO area to the University of Texas system. The cleanup has cost some $80 million, and Robert Puga, the Project Navigator trustee who was in charge of the remediation, spoke of the possibility of the sale of the 460-acre site. He spoke in front of what was described as an ASARCO community meeting, a community which, though small, obviously still sees itself as a community. An August *El Paso Inc.* editorial notes that Puga has expressed the "desire to see UTEP acquire the site's 458 acres." Puga is also quoted as saying that while he has overseen many projects, this one is a highlight for many reasons but mostly because of the high level of community interest. "Through it all, the one thing that struck me was how polite and civil the people of El Paso were—even when they didn't agree," he explained. And it is that special quality of "communidad" which has lived on after the physical site is gone.

The sense of community has never left those families who once lived in or were associated with Smeltertown. As we have noted before, every year there are reunions or commemoration activities such as the climb up Christo Rey. Perhaps the message is that though the physical place is gone, Esmeltianos will never say "Adios" to Smeltertown.

Afterword

When I moved to El Paso and began teaching at UTEP in 1991, I was struck by the number of students and townspeople who told me elaborate stories about their families' origins. Commonly, people recounted how "my grandmother was a Tarahumara Indian who wore long black braids and my grandfather was a blond, blue-eyed Spaniard." Others reminisced about Pancho Villa and the violence of the Mexican Revolution that caused their families to leave Chihuahua and cross the US border. The other story I heard repeatedly recalled family roots in the copper-refining community of Smeltertown. Whereas the tales of Pancho Villa invariably separated into those who blamed him for brutality or trying to kidnap a female relative, or praised Villa for rising up against oppression, the descendants of Smeltertown uniformly spoke of their great pride in the town and their family's success. They attributed their prosperity to the ferocious work ethic of their relatives at the refinery. No doubt other border residents preserve less happy memories of Smeltertown, ones emphasizing inequality, mistreatment, and pollution. But for whatever reason, their stories never reached me. Pride of place and community and the economic betterment associated with industrial labor overpowered a sense of social and environmental injustice in the minds of the Smeltertown relatives I met in my classes and in the Juárez/El Paso area.

Due to my focus on other border research questions, I was never able to collect the stories I heard about the community in a systematic way. Yet Smeltertown, which like Bisbee, Douglas, and Clifton-Morenci, Arizona, is one of the greatest company towns in US history, merits further study. Thanks to Marcia Hatfield Daudistel, Mimi R. Gladstein, and Carol Eastman, we now have a verbatim account of the women of Smeltertown to complement previous historical research. Oral histories, direct testimonies of the lives and feelings of the Smeltertown women, form the core of this fine book. As Monica Perales points out, "The story of Smeltertown is fundamentally one steeped in memory, shrouded in a foggy mix of nostalgia, myth, and misperception."[11]

Renowned Africanist Jan Vansina considered oral tradition, in fact, as a form of history, especially among the rural African people whose stories he compiled for decades. Svetlana Alexievich, winner of the 2015 Nobel Prize for literature, is considered a master of the oral history approach and is even credited with the creation of a new genre of literature: "a history of emotions," which consists of a "carefully composed collage of human voices."[12] As Orlando Figes has noted in relation to the histories of Russian women collected by Alexievich:

> Women tend to remember differently from men—a difference noted by psychologists and oral historians alike. They are better at recording their feelings. They talk more freely about them than men, who focus more on actions and the sequence of events . . . [13]

These pithy observations resonate with the Smeltertown women's stories collected by Marcia Hatfield Daudistel and Mimi Gladstein. The women of Smeltertown seldom obtained work in formal or high-paying jobs but mostly engaged in child care and domestic roles. When employed, it was usually as maids or clerks, as workers in laundries, garment factories, or hospitals, or in the ASARCO Smelter during World War II. Despite formidable race, class, and gender barriers, the Mexican and Mexican-American women of Smeltertown successfully negotiated and navigated two systems (American and Mexican) of gender expectations. They kept the community strong both within their households and in the larger society, while blending and creating new identities for themselves through education, clothing and style, and biculturalism. Like their "smelter men" counterparts, the women felt a deep connection to their community and its customs, which is still today passed on through oral tradition.

Smeltertown women's efforts to maintain homes and strengthen community life consisted of myriad quotidian tasks and countless hours of often unobserved and loyal, selfless service. Besides tending to the children and elderly, healing with herbs and other remedies, and cooking and cleaning, women gave color and flavor to the town through planting flowers, growing gardens, tidying up such public spaces as the nearby cemetery, and adorning the home inside and out. They also developed unique clothing, hair, and other beauty-related motifs, and sewn and embroidered textiles that brightened life in the brown and drab desert and the stark streets of a company town soiled with industrial dust and air pollution. Women developed small cottage industries, stores, and informal eateries to nourish school kids, teachers, and workers in the smelter. They were the glue that held together church and other social institutions, clubs, and civic activities outside the home.

The tremendous pride and seemingly perplexing loyalty to ASARCO that former Smeltertown residents and descendants express is a result of the fact that though relatively poor and exploited, Smeltertown workers and their families nevertheless formed a kind of local upper working class. While poor, they were somewhat better off than the throngs of impoverished people in the nearby hardscrabble barrios of Juárez just across the Rio Grande/Río Bravo, and the underemployed and underpaid Chicano laborers of downtown El Paso. Yet Smeltertown denizens were clearly social inferiors to the white managerial class of Smelter Terrace and the Anglo-Saxon middle classes of El Paso. Indeed, Smeltertown women were at the center of the competing centripetal and centrifugal pressures of migration, nationality, class, ethnicity, and religion that pushed and pulled Mexican Americans in divergent directions and placed Smeltertown above or below various groups in the local social hierarchy. In such a setting, consumption of particular foods, whether tacos and tortillas or hamburgers and bread; distinctive clothing styles ("Mexican" blouses vs. US upper garments); and the speaking of Spanish or English were all carefully observed markers of social distinctions.

The interviews with smelter women of the managerial class provide a revealing window onto an apartheid-like segregation in which white women lived in large, comfortable modern homes and seldom or never set foot in the barrio of the workers. One informant, Peggy Walters, observed: "I never went to Smeltertown, and I assume my mother did not either. There was no interaction between the workers' and management children." They enjoyed an idyllic park-like setting, with cheap maids from Juárez, in the shadow of the refinery smokestacks. Yet the Smelter Terrace girls and women also lived in a somewhat insular village with an artificial lake, socially separate though connected to the rest of El Paso proper. In any case, the white neighborhood of Smelter Terrace clearly exuded a hyper-American cultural aura, and superior economic standing, in opposition to the Mexican workers' neighborhoods. Furthermore, Anglo-American dominance was reinforced in schools where English was compulsory: " . . . the teachers were talking to us and it was like, 'what is she saying?' So if we asked each other [in Spanish], we'd get the ruler, you're supposed to speak English. Well, we didn't know how to speak English. So we either learned or we died" (Alicia Sarmiento Ramirez).

The barrio-like conditions of the Mexican workers' settlements—crowded, small, adobe and block or brick homes with few amenities—contrasted markedly with the comforts of the white managerial class. "All of the houses were made from adobe; the only thing that separated one family from the other was an adobe wall, so you could hear noise right and left from the other houses" (Dolores Lozano Jasso). Yet Smeltertown women loved their communities, which often had unique, appealing features of their own such as close ties and a nurturing village atmosphere. Additionally, despite the dirt and fumes of industry, Smeltertown nestled comfortably amidst the natural beauty of the Rio Grande/Río Bravo, picturesque Juárez, and the Mexican mountains. Dolores Romero remembered: "I have five sisters and . . . we used to have all kinds of food around; we had chickens; we had fresh eggs; we had rabbits. And Skull Canyon [La

Calavera neighborhood area] was a beautiful place. It had different flora and fauna."

As Perales has explained, myths and legendary images of Smeltertown have a life of their own that is interwoven with social history, and they have become social "facts" for Smeltertown descendants. Romantic images of the hearty aroma of red chile and beans and the pleasures of a tight-knit community should not prevent us from understanding how poorly the smelter workers were paid, how unfairly they and their families were treated, or how the copper refinery wreaked ecological destruction. Recently UTEP bought the land where Smeltertown and the ASARCO refinery once prospered. Let us hope that the university will carry on the best traditions of Smeltertown, and keep its mistreatment of workers and its environmental pollution buried, though not forgotten, in the past.

Howard Campbell
Professor of Anthropology
The University of Texas at El Paso

Notes

1. *The Handbook of Texas* Online.

2. Perales, Monica. *Smeltertown: Making and Remembering a Southwest Border Community.* The University of North Carolina Press, 2010.

3. Craver, Rebecca, and Adair Margo. *Tom Lea: An Oral History.* Texas Western Press, 1995.

4. "Their Mines, Our Stories: Work, Environment and Justice in ASAR-CO–Impacted Communities" (www.theirminesourstories).

5. Armenta, Manny. *United Steelworkers News.* November 10, 2009.

6. LaVenture, Bob. *United Steelworkers News.* November 10, 2009.

7. Armenta, Manny. *United Steelworkers News.* November 10, 2009.

8. Perales, Monica. *Smeltertown.*

9. De Santos, Elena. *Smeltertown, Texas.* Personal memoir.

10. Perales, Monica. *Smeltertown.*

11. Perales, Monica. *Smeltertown.*

12. Figes, Orlando. "Alexievich's New Kind of History." The New York Review of Books Vol. LXIII, No. 15, pp. 18–19, October 13, 2016.

13. Vansina, Jan. *Oral Tradition as History.* Madison: University of Wisconsin Press, 1985.

About the Authors

Marcia Hatfield Daudistel is most recently the coauthor, with writer and photographer Bill Wright, of *Authentic Texas: People of the Big Bend,* winner of the 2014 Southwest Book Award of the Border Regional Library Association. She is the editor of *Grace and Gumption: the Women of El Paso,* winner of a 2013 San Antonio Conservation Society publication award, and *Literary El Paso,* winner of the 2010 Southwest Book Award of the Border Regional Library Association, both published by TCU Press.

She was selected as the recipient of the 2012 Literary Legacy Award from El Paso Community College and is a 2013 inductee into the El Paso Commission for Women Hall of Fame. She also serves on the Friends of the Jeff Davis County Library Board. Marcia is a member of the Texas Institute of Letters.

Mimi Reisel Gladstein is a professor of English at the University of Texas at El Paso and has chaired both English and the Theatre and Dance Departments. She is the author of five books and coeditor of two. *The Last Supper of Chicano Heroes: Selected Works of José Antonio Burciaga,* co-edited with Daniel Chacon, won an American Book Award, a Southwest Book Award, and a Latino Book Award. Gladstein's scholarly articles have been translated and published in both Mexico and Japan.

International recognition includes the John J. and Angeline Pruis Award for teaching Steinbeck and the Burkhardt Award for Steinbeck scholarship. Named to the El Paso Commission for Women Hall of Fame in 2011, she has also been inducted into the El Paso County Historical Society Hall of Honor.

Carol Eastman is an award-winning photographer whose work has been published and exhibited locally, nationally, and internationally. It is held by the Texas Tech Medical School, the El Paso Holocaust Museum, and the University of Texas Special Collections Library. Her work has been supported by US Department of Commerce, Museum of Northern Arizona, and Northern Arizona University for a video and catalogs on Native American art; by the Texas Commission on the Arts, El Paso Museum and Department, and

National Park Service for "Children of the Border"; by the El Paso Museum of History for "Traces"; by Northern Arizona University and the National Science Foundation for a video on Native American education; and by the El Paso Community Foundation for illustrations of New Mexico ranchers.